MAIN-COURSE SALADS

MAIN-COURSE SALADS

RAY OVERTON

PHOTOGRAPHS BY BRAD NEWTON

LONGSTREET
Atlanta, Georgia

This book is dedicated with love and admiration to my assistant and forever friend, Susan Montgomery. Thanks for doing the things you do!

Published by
LONGSTREET PRESS, INC.
A subsidiary of Cox Newspapers,
A subsidiary of Cox Enterprises, Inc.
2140 Newmarket Parkway
Suite 122
Marietta, GA 30067

Printed in the United States of America
2nd printing, revised, 1999
Library of Congress Catalog Card Number: 99-60107
ISBN: 1-56352-512-7

Book and jacket design by Burtch Bennett Hunter

CONTENTS

INTRODUCTION

In the past few years, salads have come into their own. No longer content to be an opening act or supporting player, they are now taking center stage. And why not? Main-course salads are full of the flavorful, fresh, and healthy ingredients we have come to associate with good eating: assorted greens, vibrant herbs, lean meats and poultry, bakery breads, farmhouse cheeses, roasted vegetables, and fresh fruits. A meal in a bowl is an appealing idea in today's busy world, when multi-course meals – especially during the week – are a thing of the past. And with such a diversity of greens and other ingredients available in today's supermarkets, salads are a welcome choice in any season.

GREENS

A few tips on preparation and storage are all you need to ensure fresh greens in your salads. I usually wash my lettuces as soon as I get home from the market, swishing them in several changes of water until all the sand and grit are gone. (Nothing can ruin the taste of a delicious salad more quickly than a single piece of grit.) Next, I thoroughly dry the greens. An indispensable kitchen accessory is a salad spinner, a contraption that uses centrifugal force to remove excess moisture. I usually prep my greens immediately after by removing stems or large ribs and tearing larger leaves into bite-sized pieces. To store the greens, wrap them in a paper towel and place in vegetable zip-top bags (those perforated bags with small holes that balance the humidity level inside). Place the bags in the refrigerator crisper, on top of heavier items such as apples or citrus fruit. Prepped and stored in this manner, greens will usually last a good week. Some of the more common greens available today include:

- Arugula - small, dark green leaves with a slightly bitter, peppery taste. Also known as rocket or rugula and often found in the herb section of the grocery store.

- Belgian endive - These spear-shaped heads of tightly-packed, whitish yellow leaves have a faintly bitter taste. For a milder taste, choose those with a more yellowy tinge.

1

- Bok choy - crisp Asian cabbage with large white ribs and dark green leaves.

- Boston lettuce - Also called butter or bibb lettuce, it has a very soft texture and sweet flavor.

- Cabbage – Choose red, green, or Napa. The latter is elongated, with frilly leaves, and has a wonderful affinity for Asian-inspired salads.

- Curly endive - Also known by its French name, frisée, or the more common term, chicory, this lettuce has frilly, dark green leaves and is very bitter. The lighter-colored inner leaves are milder in taste.

- Escarole - Related to chicory, this green has broader leaves but the same characteristic bitter taste.

- Iceberg lettuce – Virtually tasteless but refreshingly crisp, it makes an excellent base for a number of salads. Once ubiquitous in American salads, then maligned by many culinary professionals, iceberg is now enjoying a well-deserved comeback.

- Mesclun - From the French word for "mixture," mesclun is a term used for a combination of mixed baby greens and herbs (sometimes packaged as "spring mix" or "California mix"). Components may include red romaine, green romaine, red and green leaf lettuce, green mustard, baby spinach, Swiss chard, radicchio, frisée, arugula, mâche, dandelion, red and green oak leaf, watercress, baby Asian greens such as bok choy, mizuna, or tat soi, and herbs such as chervil, basil, or sorrel. Because the greens are carefully harvested when very small and tender, mesclun is usually expensive, but it is well worth it for the vast flavor it yields.

- Oak leaf lettuce - Green or edged with red, these tender, very mild, sweet greens resemble oak leaves.

- Radicchio - looks like a small, compact head of cabbage, red to purple in color, with very white ribs and a unique, bitter taste.

- Romaine - long, narrow leaves and a very sweet flavor. It's the only choice for Caesar salad.

- Spinach - Young spinach has very tender, very dark green leaves with a slightly astringent taste. Make sure the leaves are cleaned very well, as they tend to harbor grit in their crinkly leaves. Remove the stems from older (and larger) spinach. Spinach can stand up to very assertive dressings and warm vinaigrettes, used to slightly wilt the greens.

- Watercress - A spicy, peppery green with a smaller leaf than arugula, it can be substituted for arugula in any of these recipes.

Each recipe yields four very generous main-course servings. In most cases, you need only a spectacular bread and some liquid refreshment to round out the meal. When choosing a wine, a good rule of thumb is to match it with the vinegar in the salad. If the dressing or vinaigrette calls for a champagne vinegar, white wine vinegar, apple cider vinegar, or fruit-infused vinegar, I would go with a chardonnay or pinot grigio. When using a red wine vinegar, balsamic vinegar, or sherry vinegar, choose a hearty merlot or full-bodied cabernet. Spicier salads go well with ice-cold beer, both foreign and domestic.

Each recipe yields more dressing than you probably need. I like to dress my salads using about ¼ cup of vinaigrette for 4 cups of salad. Save a little back. If the salad appears too dry, add the remaining dressing. Otherwise, pass it separately at the table.

Finally, when you are inventing your own main-course salads, remember the following guidelines:

Match assertive greens (such as arugula, spinach, radicchio, and Belgian endive) with strong-flavored dressings and hearty ingredients such as beef, ham, or sausage. Milder greens require a subtle vinaigrette.

Mesclun topped with crisp-tender sautéed vegetables and grilled seafood, poultry, lamb, or pork is instantly transformed into a main-meal salad. Top with any of the vinaigrette recipes in this book, or opt for good-quality bottled dressing.

Salads using pasta, rice, potatoes, bread, or a grain as the main ingredient are always best when served at room temperature. If you make the salad ahead, let it sit out of the refrigerator for at least 1 hour before serving.

Experiment with contrasting temperatures and textures, such as warm goat cheese on frilly green leaves or crunchy apple wedges with wilted greens.

For composed or layered salads, use ingredients cut to similar size and weight so they will be evenly dispersed throughout the salad and evenly coated with the dressing.

PICNIC SALADS
(SALADS TO GO)

Curried Chicken and Wild Rice Salad with Pita Crisps

Citrus Chicken Salad with Sun-Dried Tomato Vinaigrette

Antipasto Salad with Pesto Vinaigrette

Southwestern Black Bean Salad with Queso Cheese and Chili Lime Vinaigrette

Summer Lentil Salad with Toasted Cumin Vinaigrette

Fresh Tuna Salad with Golden Raisins and Cashews

Chickpea, Pasta, and Tuna Toss

Fiery Thai Beef Salad with Lemongrass Vinaigrette

Marinated Broccoli Salad with Grated Cheese and Dried Cranberries

Cracked Wheat, Barley, and Diced Pork Salad

Corn and Butter Pea Salad with Glazed Country Ham

Jamaican Jerked Pork Salad with Rice and Peas

CURRIED CHICKEN & WILD RICE SALAD WITH PITA CRISPS

Control the degree of heat for this recipe by choosing mild or hot curry powder. If the label doesn't specify, check the ingredients: the hotter the blend, the closer cayenne or ground red pepper will be to the top of the list.

SERVES 4

2 cups coarsely chopped cooked chicken

2 cups cooked wild rice

½ cup mango chutney, preferably Major Grey's

2 tablespoons butter

2 tablespoons olive oil

1 onion, finely chopped

2 garlic cloves, finely chopped

1 tablespoon hot or mild curry powder, preferably Madras

1 cup dried cranberries

½ cup golden raisins

½ cup mayonnaise

½ cup sour cream

½ cup sunflower seeds

2 Golden Delicious apples, cored and cut into small chunks

¼ cup chopped fresh parsley

2 tablespoons lemon juice

Salt and freshly ground black pepper

2 cups torn radicchio

1 small head red leaf lettuce, torn into bite-sized
   pieces (about 4 cups)

1 small head green leaf lettuce, torn into bite-sized
   pieces (about 4 cups)

In a large bowl combine the chicken, wild rice, and mango chutney. Mix well and set aside.

In a 12-inch skillet or sauté pan over medium-high heat, melt the butter with the olive oil until hot. Add the onion and garlic. Cook, stirring often until the onions begin to wilt, about 5 minutes. Stir in the curry powder and cook for 2 minutes. Remove from the heat and stir in the cranberries, raisins, mayonnaise, sour cream, sunflower seeds, apples, parsley, lemon juice, and salt and pepper to taste. Stir mixture into the chicken and wild rice. Cover and refrigerate for at least 2 hours or overnight.

In a large bowl toss together the radicchio, red leaf lettuce, and green leaf lettuce. When ready to serve, arrange greens on a large platter. Mound the curried chicken mixture in the center of the greens. Surround with Pita Crisps (recipe follows) and serve at once.

Variation: For a picnic sandwich, split 6 (6 inch) whole-wheat pita rounds in half. Open the pockets and fill each half with some of the greens and curried chicken mixture. The pita pocket sandwiches can be made ahead and refrigerated, tightly wrapped in plastic wrap, up to 4 hours before serving.

PITA CRISPS

MAKES ABOUT 32 CRISPS

4 (6 inch) whole-wheat pita rounds, cut into quarters
and separated
⅓ cup olive oil
2 garlic cloves, chopped
1 tablespoon chopped fresh rosemary
½ teaspoon red pepper flakes
½ cup freshly grated Parmesan cheese

Preheat the oven to 400°F.

Place the pita wedges on a large baking sheet. In a small bowl combine the olive oil, garlic, rosemary, and red pepper flakes. Lightly brush each wedge with some of the oil mixture. Sprinkle with the Parmesan cheese. Bake until crisp, 8 to 10 minutes. Remove from the oven and allow to cool. Store in an airtight container for 4 to 5 days, or freeze for up to 1 month.

CITRUS CHICKEN SALAD WITH SUN-DRIED TOMATO VINAIGRETTE

4 boneless, skinless chicken breasts

Juice and grated zest of 2 oranges

Juice and grated zest of 2 lemons

Juice and grated zest of 2 limes

½ cup oil-packed sun-dried tomatoes, drained

2 garlic cloves

⅓ cup seasoned breadcrumbs

¼ cup balsamic vinegar

½ cup extra-virgin olive oil

2 tablespoons fresh thyme leaves

1 teaspoon sugar

Salt and freshly ground black pepper

6 cups mesclun or assorted baby lettuces

4 Belgian endive, bottom cores removed, thinly sliced
    lengthwise, and separated into strands

1 cup alfalfa sprouts

½ cup grated Romano cheese

⅔ cup toasted pine nuts (see note)

Place the boneless, skinless chicken breasts in a large bowl. Add the citrus juices and zests and let marinate at room temperature for 1 hour. Preheat the broiler. Place the chicken on a foil-lined baking sheet and cook for 15 to 18 minutes, turning the chicken once. Transfer the chicken to a cutting board and cut into thin strips. Set aside.

In a food processor combine the sun-dried tomatoes, garlic, breadcrumbs, balsamic vinegar, olive oil, thyme leaves, sugar, and salt and pepper to taste. Process until vinaigrette is thick and emulsified.

In a large bowl toss together the mesclun or assorted baby lettuces and Belgian endive. Toss with half of the vinaigrette. Divide among 4 serving plates. Top the lettuces with the sliced chicken and drizzle with the remaining vinaigrette. Garnish each serving with alfalfa sprouts, Romano cheese, and pine nuts.

Note: To toast nuts, preheat the oven to 350°F. Place the nuts on a baking sheet and toast, stirring occasionally, for 6 to 10 minutes. The older the nut is, the more quickly it will toast. I store nuts in my freezer, dated and labeled, in a heavy-duty zip-top freezer bag, for up to 9 months.

Variation: To serve this salad as an appetizer, separate the Belgian endive into individual spears. Finely chop the chicken and toss with the vinaigrette. Stir in the Romano cheese and pine nuts. Spread about 1 tablespoon of the chicken mixture on each endive spear. Top each with some of the alfalfa sprouts. Place on a serving platter in a circular design (to resemble the petals of a flower). Refrigerate until ready to serve. These can be made up to a day ahead and stored, tightly wrapped.

ANTIPASTO SALAD
WITH PESTO VINAIGRETTE

If you need to save time, use a good quality prepared pesto sauce. This vinaigrette also is ideal for basting for grilled vegetables.

SERVES 4

1 tablespoon Dijon mustard

2 garlic cloves, chopped

¼ cup balsamic vinegar

⅓ cup Homemade Pesto Sauce (recipe follows)

½ cup olive oil

Salt and freshly ground black pepper

8 ounces uncooked fusilli

1 cup broccoli florets

1 red bell pepper, seeded and cut into julienne strips

1 green bell pepper, seeded and cut into julienne strips

1 cup pitted and sliced black kalamata olives

¼ pound pepperoni slices

1 cup mozzarella, cut into ½-inch cubes

1 cup freshly grated Parmesan cheese, divided

In a large bowl whisk together the mustard, garlic, balsamic vinegar, and pesto sauce. Slowly whisk in the olive oil. Taste for seasoning and add salt and pepper as needed. Set aside.

Cook the fusilli in boiling salted water for 8 to 10 minutes. Drain, rinse with cold water, and drain again. Add to the bowl with the vinaigrette. Stir in the broccoli, red and green bell pepper strips, and black olives. Add the pepperoni slices, mozzarella, and ½ cup of the Parmesan cheese. Cover and refrigerate until ready to serve, at least 2 hours or up to 2 days. Just before serving, sprinkle with the remaining Parmesan cheese.

HOMEMADE PESTO SAUCE

Use this pesto sauce as a spread on breads; tossed with pasta or steamed vegetables; stirred into soups and stews; added to a vinaigrette; to baste grilled vegetables, salmon, or chicken; or stirred into a risotto.

MAKES ABOUT 1 CUP

2 cups firmly packed basil leaves (about 2 bunches),
   washed and dried

3 garlic cloves, finely chopped

¼ cup toasted chopped walnuts or pine nuts (see page 9)

½ teaspoon salt

½ teaspoon black pepper

½ cup freshly grated Parmesan cheese

½ cup extra-virgin olive oil

Process the basil leaves, garlic, walnuts or pine nuts, salt, pepper, and Parmesan cheese in a food processor until smooth, scraping down the sides of the bowl as necessary. With the machine running, slowly pour in the olive oil until it is thoroughly incorporated and the pesto is smooth.

Store in the refrigerator, lightly covered with a thin layer of olive oil, for 1 week, or freeze for up to 1 month. If you are going to freeze it, place it in an airtight container and press a piece of plastic wrap onto the surface of the sauce before sealing the lid to discourage darkening of the sauce.

SOUTHWESTERN BLACK BEAN SALAD WITH QUESO CHEESE & CHILI LIME VINAIGRETTE

This salad and dressing can be made a day ahead and refrigerated, making it perfect for picnics or casual Sunday night suppers. For better flavor and texture, toss the salad with the vinaigrette just before serving. This combination is also delicious wrapped in warm flour tortillas and eaten out of hand.

SERVES 4

1 (15½ ounce) can black beans, rinsed and drained

8 tomatillos, husks removed, rinsed, and thinly sliced

4 plum tomatoes, thinly sliced crosswise

1 red onion, chopped

4 green onions, chopped

2 garlic cloves, chopped

1 (15½ ounce) can yellow corn, rinsed and drained

1 English cucumber, cut in half lengthwise, seeded, and finely diced

3 jalapeño peppers, seeded and chopped

2 cups broken or crushed tortilla chips

1½ cups crumbled Queso or finely grated Monterey Jack cheese

Juice of 4 limes

1 tablespoon chili powder

2 teaspoons ground cumin

½ teaspoon ground coriander

½ cup chopped fresh cilantro

½ cup peanut oil

Salt and freshly ground black pepper

½ cup pepitas (pumpkin seeds) or sunflower seeds, toasted (see page 9)

In a large, clear glass bowl, layer the black beans, tomatillos, plum tomatoes, red onion, green onions, garlic, corn, cucumber, jalapeño peppers, tortilla chips, and cheese.

In a small bowl whisk together the lime juice, chili powder, cumin, coriander, and cilantro. Whisk in the peanut oil in a thin, steady stream and add salt and pepper to taste.

Bring the layered salad and vinaigrette to the table. Just before serving, drizzle the vinaigrette over the salad and toss to coat completely. Garnish with the pepitas or sunflower seeds. Serve at once.

SUMMER LENTIL SALAD WITH TOASTED CUMIN VINAIGRETTE

If you like, double the amount of vinaigrette and use the extra to baste grilled chicken, pork, or salmon.
Cube or shred the meat and add to the salad just before tossing.

SERVES 4

2½ cups green or brown lentils, washed
    and picked over (see note)
1 quart chicken stock
2 bay leaves
1 tablespoon crushed cumin seeds
¼ cup freshly squeezed lemon juice
1 tablespoon Dijon mustard
2 garlic cloves, chopped
Salt and freshly ground black pepper
Sugar to taste
½ cup extra-virgin olive oil
1 cup chopped fresh parsley
1 onion, chopped
2 red bell peppers, seeded and chopped
2 ribs of celery, chopped
2 carrots, shredded
1 tablespoon chopped fresh rosemary
½ (10 ounce) package pre-washed spinach, stems removed
    (about 6 cups)
4 ounces sharp cheddar cheese, cut into strips
2 cups store-bought salad croutons

In a 3½-quart Dutch oven combine the lentils, chicken stock, and bay leaves. Bring to a boil, reduce the heat to medium, and simmer, covered, for 30 minutes, or until the lentils are tender. Drain any excess liquid and discard the bay leaves. Place the lentils in a large bowl to cool.

In a 6-inch skillet over medium-high heat toast the cumin seeds until they just begin to smoke, about 1 minute. In a small bowl whisk together the cumin seeds, lemon juice, Dijon mustard, garlic, and salt, pepper, and sugar to taste. Add the olive oil in a thin, steady stream until the dressing is thick and emulsified. Set aside.

To the cooled lentils add the parsley, onion, red bell pepper, celery, carrots, and rosemary. Drizzle with the vinaigrette and toss to coat. Line a large platter with spinach leaves and place the lentil salad on top. Garnish with cheddar cheese strips and croutons.

Note: To save time, you can substitute 2 (15½ ounce) cans of lentils (rinsed and drained) for the dried variety. (Omit the chicken stock and bay leaves in the recipe.) I've also enjoyed this salad with a combination of canned black beans and yellow corn replacing the lentils.

FRESH TUNA SALAD
WITH GOLDEN RAISINS & CASHEWS

You can substitute 3 cans of chunk white albacore tuna packed in spring water and drained for the fresh tuna. Sometimes I serve this tuna salad with large, whole leaves of Bibb lettuce so guests can fill and roll the lettuce and enjoy without the constraints of a fork and plate. This variation works very well for outdoor dining occasions such as beach picnics or concerts in the park.

SERVES 4

4 (6 ounce) tuna steaks

½ cup plus 2 tablespoons freshly squeezed lemon juice

2 tablespoons olive oil

Salt and freshly ground black pepper

1 small Vidalia onion, chopped

2 ribs of celery, chopped

1 carrot, shredded

2 hard-cooked eggs, chopped

1 cup mayonnaise

1 tablespoon capers, rinsed and drained

½ cup golden raisins

⅔ cup chopped lightly salted cashews

3 tablespoons chopped fresh tarragon

4 large vine-ripened tomatoes, cored and thinly sliced

3 green onions, chopped

Preheat the broiler. Place the tuna steaks in a shallow glass baking dish. In a small bowl whisk together ½ cup of the lemon juice, olive oil, and salt and pepper to taste. Pour over the tuna steaks. Marinate at room temperature, uncovered, for 30 minutes, turning the steaks after 15 minutes. Place the tuna steaks on a foil-lined baking sheet and broil for 3 to 4 minutes per side, turning once. Remove from the oven and cut into ½-inch pieces.

In a large bowl combine the diced tuna, onion, celery, carrot, hard-cooked eggs, mayonnaise, the remaining 2 tablespoons lemon juice, capers, golden raisins, cashews, and tarragon.

Line 4 individual serving plates with the sliced tomato. Lightly season the tomato slices with salt and pepper. Mound the tuna salad in the middle of each plate, top with green onions, and serve at once.

CHICKPEA, PASTA, & TUNA TOSS

If your pantry is well stocked there's no advance planning to this meal on the go — it's ready in about 15 minutes.

*3 (6 ounce) cans chunk white albacore tuna in spring
  water, drained*

1 (15½ ounce) can chickpeas, rinsed and drained

*8 ounces shell-shaped pasta, cooked according to package
  directions and drained*

1 small yellow onion, chopped

2 ribs of celery, chopped

1 carrot, shredded

2 hard-cooked eggs, chopped

1 cup mayonnaise

2 tablespoons apple cider vinegar

3 tablespoons chopped fresh basil

Salt and freshly ground black pepper

6 cups baby spinach leaves, washed and dried

4 vine-ripened tomatoes, cored and quartered

3 green onions, chopped

In a large bowl combine the tuna, chickpeas, pasta, onion, celery, carrot, hard-cooked eggs, mayonnaise, apple cider vinegar, basil, and salt and pepper to taste.

Line 4 individual serving plates with the baby spinach leaves. Mound the tuna salad in the middle of each plate, surround with the quartered tomatoes, and top with the green onions. Serve at once.

FIERY THAI BEEF SALAD WITH LEMONGRASS VINAIGRETTE

This is a wonderful salad, full of bright flavors and interesting textures. It is also an excellent way to use up leftover beef. My assistant and dear friend, Susan Montgomery, and her husband, Mike, often take this salad to Turner Stadium when the Atlanta Braves have a home game. It sure beats ballpark hot dogs and peanuts.

SERVES 4

1½ pounds cooked beef tenderloin, London broil, or sirloin steak, very thinly sliced

6 green onions, sliced on the diagonal in ½-inch slices

2 shallots, chopped

½ cup coarsely chopped fresh cilantro

¼ cup beef stock

⅓ cup fish sauce

⅓ cup freshly squeezed lime juice

1 tablespoon brown sugar

1 teaspoon red pepper flakes

1 tablespoon finely chopped lemongrass (see note)

2 tablespoons chile oil

Romaine lettuce

1 English cucumber, halved lengthwise and thinly sliced on the diagonal

1 pint cherry tomatoes, halved

⅓ cup tightly packed fresh mint leaves

Place the beef in a large mixing bowl. Add the green onions, shallots, and cilantro.

Make the lemongrass vinaigrette: In a small bowl whisk together the beef stock, fish sauce, lime juice, brown sugar, red pepper flakes, lemon grass, and chile oil. Add to the beef and toss well to thoroughly combine. Let marinate at room temperature for 20 minutes.

Line a large platter with Romaine lettuce leaves. With a slotted spoon transfer the beef to the platter. Arrange the cucumber slices and cherry tomato halves around the beef. Drizzle with the vinaigrette. Scatter the mint leaves on top.

Note: To prepare lemongrass, cut off the base of the bulb and trim away the dried outer leaves. Use only the bottom 2 inches of the lemongrass. Coarsely chop the bulb and then pound slightly with the broad side of a knife to release the essential citronella oils. Finely chop and use as directed.

MARINATED BROCCOLI SALAD WITH GRATED CHEESE & DRIED CRANBERRIES

This down-home delight can be made ahead in stages and refrigerated for up to 2 days, making it the perfect dish for a Fourth of July picnic, church supper, or easy Sunday night with the remote control in hand. About an hour before serving, toss the dressing with the vegetables and top with the garnishes. Diced ham makes a nice alternative to the chicken or turkey.

SERVES 4

2 cups shredded cooked chicken or turkey

1 head of broccoli, cut into florets

1 red onion, chopped

1 red bell pepper, seeded and chopped

1 green bell pepper, seeded and chopped

1 yellow bell pepper, seeded and chopped

2 carrots, shredded

1 cup sliced button mushrooms

1 cup lightly toasted sunflower seeds (see page 9)

1 cup dried cranberries

1 cup mayonnaise

⅓ cup red wine vinegar

¼ cup sugar

Salt and freshly ground black pepper

8 slices of bacon, chopped, fried until golden brown, and drained, divided

1 cup finely grated cheddar cheese, divided

In a large bowl mix together the shredded chicken or turkey, broccoli, red onion, red bell pepper, green bell pepper, yellow bell pepper, carrots, mushrooms, sunflower seeds, and dried cranberries. Toss to mix completely.

In a medium bowl combine the mayonnaise, red wine vinegar, sugar, and salt and pepper to taste.

About 1 hour before serving, toss the vegetables with the dressing. Add half of the bacon and grated cheese and toss once more. Transfer to a serving platter. Sprinkle with the remaining bacon and cheese. Serve at once.

CRACKED WHEAT, BARLEY, & DICED PORK SALAD

Toasting the barley in butter gives this dish a rich, nutty flavor. Four boneless, skinless chicken breasts can be substituted for the pork. For a totally vegetarian dish, omit the pork and use vegetable stock instead of chicken stock.

SERVES 4

½ cup cracked wheat (bulgur)

2 cups boiling water

4 tablespoons butter

2 cups medium pearl barley, rinsed and drained

4 cups chicken stock

1 cup dry white wine

1½ pounds pork tenderloin, cut into ¾-inch cubes

Salt and freshly ground black pepper

6 shallots, thinly sliced

3 plum tomatoes, seeded and diced

2 jalapeño peppers, seeded and finely minced

2 carrots, shredded

1 cup thinly sliced button mushrooms

⅓ cup freshly squeezed lemon juice

⅓ cup extra-virgin olive oil

1 cup assorted chopped fresh herbs, such as basil, parsley,
    mint, rosemary, and oregano

⅔ cup crumbled feta cheese

Assorted fresh herb sprigs for garnish

In a large bowl combine the cracked wheat with the boiling water and let stand for 2 hours. Drain well and return cracked wheat to the bowl.

In a 3½-quart Dutch oven with a tight-fitting lid, melt the butter over medium heat. Add the barley and cook, stirring often, until the barley starts to brown and gives off a rich, nutty aroma, about 10 minutes. Add the chicken stock, white wine, pork, and salt and pepper to taste. Bring to a boil, then reduce the heat to a simmer. Cover and cook for about 45 minutes, or until the liquid has been absorbed. Transfer to the bowl with the drained cracked wheat.

Add the shallots, tomatoes, jalapeño peppers, carrots, mushrooms, lemon juice, olive oil, and chopped herbs. Toss to coat completely. Transfer to a large serving platter and sprinkle with the feta cheese. Garnish with the fresh herb sprigs. Serve at once.

CORN & BUTTER PEA SALAD WITH GLAZED COUNTRY HAM

This easy and delicious summer salad recipe is a variation of one I enjoyed as a child. If at all possible, try to use fresh corn and butter peas, although even the frozen ones work well if you get a craving in the mid-winter months.

SERVES 4

6 ears fresh white corn, kernels scraped from the cob (see note), or 1½ (16 ounce) packages frozen shoepeg corn

16 ounces shelled butter peas or petite lima beans or 1 (16 ounce) package frozen butter peas or petite lima beans

2 thin slices Smithfield country ham (or other smoked and cured ham)

½ cup Coca-Cola (do not use diet)

6 slices of bacon, chopped

1 Vidalia onion, finely chopped

½ cup apple cider vinegar

2 teaspoons poultry seasoning

1 cucumber, halved lengthwise, seeded, and diced

1 red bell pepper, seeded and chopped

1 cup mayonnaise

1 tablespoon fresh thyme leaves

Salt and freshly ground black pepper

4 green onions, finely chopped

Fill a 3½-quart Dutch oven with lightly salted water and bring to a boil. Add the corn and butter peas and simmer for 3 minutes, or until the vegetables are crisp-tender. Do not overcook. Drain and refresh under cold running water. Transfer to a large mixing bowl.

In a 12-inch skillet over medium-high heat, fry the country ham slices until heated through, turning once, about 2 to 3 minutes on each side. Add the Coca-Cola and simmer until the liquid has evaporated and glazed the ham. Remove the ham from the skillet and cut into bite-sized pieces.

In the same skillet set over medium-high heat, fry the bacon until golden brown. Stir in the Vidalia onion and cook just long enough to wilt the onions, about 2 minutes. Add the apple cider vinegar and cook until the liquid has been reduced by half. Stir in the poultry seasoning and set aside to cool.

To the bowl with the corn and butterpeas add the cucumber, red bell pepper, mayonnaise, and thyme leaves. Fold in the contents of the skillet and the glazed ham. Season to taste with salt and pepper.

Cover salad and chill at least 4 hours or overnight to allow the flavors to marry. Transfer to a serving platter and garnish with the chopped green onions. Serve at once. Salad will keep for 3 to 4 days in the refrigerator.

Note: The easiest way to remove the kernels from the cob is to anchor one end of a corncob on the center tube of an angel food cake pan. With a sharp knife cut the kernels straight down. The kernels will collect in the bottom of the pan instead of flying all over the kitchen counter.

JAMAICAN JERKED PORK SALAD
WITH RICE & PEAS

Be sure to use an unsweetened coconut milk for this dish. In Jamaica this classic dish is known as "peas 'n' rice" even though pinto or red beans, not peas, are used.

2 cups unsweetened coconut milk

2½ cups chicken stock

2 cups basmati rice, rinsed

1½ pounds pork tenderloin, cut into ½-inch cubes

Salt and freshly ground black pepper

¼ cup olive oil

¼ cup apple cider vinegar

¼ cup freshly squeezed orange juice

¼ cup freshly squeezed lime juice

1 tablespoon light brown sugar

2 Scotch bonnet peppers, seeded and chopped

1 tablespoon fresh thyme leaves

1 teaspoon poultry seasoning

½ teaspoon allspice

2 (15½ ounce) cans pinto beans, rinsed and drained

1 red onion, chopped

1 red bell pepper, seeded and chopped

1 carrot, shredded

½ cup chopped fresh cilantro

4 green onions, chopped

4 garlic cloves, chopped

1 head red leaf lettuce, separated into leaves

⅓ cup lightly toasted unsweetened coconut (see note)

In a 2½-quart saucepan combine the coconut milk, chicken stock, rice, pork, and salt and pepper to taste. Bring to a boil, reduce the heat to a simmer, cover, and cook for 20 minutes. Remove from the heat and let sit, covered, for 10 minutes. Transfer to a large bowl.

In a medium bowl combine the olive oil, apple cider vinegar, orange juice, lime juice, brown sugar, Scotch bonnet peppers, thyme leaves, poultry seasoning, allspice, 1 teaspoon of salt, and 1 teaspoon of black pepper. Whisk until the sugar has dissolved. Set aside.

To the rice and pork mixture stir in the pinto beans, red onion, red bell pepper, carrot, cilantro, green onions, and garlic. Add the vinaigrette and toss to coat completely. Line a large serving platter with the lettuce leaves. Mound the rice mixture on top and garnish with toasted coconut. Serve at once.

Note: Toasting the coconut enhances its flavor. Toast as you would nuts (see page 9).

LUNCH AND BRUNCH SALADS

Chutney Chicken Salad with Almonds and Grapes

Szechwan Chicken Salad with Chow Mein Noodles

Crunchy Fried Green Tomato Salad with Bacon Vinaigrette

Frisée Salad with Pears and Walnut-Crusted Goat Cheese Rounds

Devilish Egg Salad with Spinach and Bacon

Broiled Tuna Salad with Roasted Red Bell Pepper Sauce

Italian Seafood Salad

Caribbean Shrimp Salad with Cantaloupe Mango Salsa

Pickled Cucumber Crescents and Crab Salad

Poached Salmon and Sour Cream Potato Salad with Salmon Roe

Prosciutto-Wrapped Figs on Arugula and Fresh Herb Bed

Spiced Chopped Ham and Pineapple Salad with Raspberry Vinaigrette

CHUTNEY CHICKEN SALAD WITH ALMONDS & GRAPES

This wonderfully fragrant chicken salad, bursting with unexpected flavors and textures, can also be stuffed into hollowed-out cherry tomatoes for a quick and easy appetizer.

SERVES 4

4 cups coarsely chopped cooked chicken or turkey

¾ cup Cranberry Vidalia Onion Chutney (recipe follows) or mango chutney, such as Major Grey's

¾ cup mayonnaise

6 green onions, chopped

Juice and grated zest of 2 oranges

1 cup slivered almonds, toasted (see page 9)

1 cup halved or quartered seedless red or green grapes

Salt and freshly ground black pepper

4 (6 inch) round Naan or other flatbread

4 cups arugula leaves, stems removed

2 cups watercress leaves, stems removed

1 cup basil leaves

2 tablespoons extra-virgin olive oil

3 tablespoons freshly squeezed lemon juice

Additional orange zest for garnish (optional)

In a large bowl combine the chopped chicken, chutney, mayonnaise, green onions, orange juice and zest, almonds, grapes, and salt and pepper to taste. Chill, covered, for 1 hour.

If desired, warm the Naan or flatbread in the oven according to package directions.

Meanwhile, in a large bowl toss together the arugula, watercress, basil leaves, olive oil, lemon juice, and salt and pepper to taste. Place a flatbread on each of 4 individual serving plates. Arrange the arugula mixture on top of the flatbreads and mound the chicken salad on top. Garnish with additional orange zest if desired.

CRANBERRY VIDALIA ONION CHUTNEY

2 Granny Smith apples, peeled, cored, and coarsely chopped

1 Vidalia onion, thinly sliced

1 red bell pepper, seeded and chopped

2 garlic cloves, chopped

2 jalapeño peppers, seeded and finely chopped

1 tablespoon chopped fresh ginger

Grated zest of 1 orange

1 cup golden raisins

1 cup brown sugar

2 cups apple cider vinegar

2 teaspoons ground cinnamon

2 teaspoons ground cumin

2 teaspoons dry mustard

1 teaspoon salt

1 cup dried cranberries

1 (12 ounce) bag fresh or frozen cranberries, rinsed and drained

Place all ingredients except the dried cranberries and fresh or frozen cranberries in a 5$\frac{1}{2}$-quart stainless steel or enameled Dutch oven. Bring to a boil over high heat. Reduce the heat to medium-low and cook, uncovered, stirring occasionally, for 2 hours.

Add the dried and fresh or frozen cranberries and continue to cook, stirring occasionally, until the berries begin to pop and the mixture thickens, about 1 hour. Be sure to watch the mixture closely as it thickens, stirring to prevent it from sticking or scorching. Cool to room temperature and refrigerate for up to 10 days.

This chutney can also be frozen in quart-sized zip-top freezer bags for up to 6 months. Defrost overnight in the refrigerator before using. Refrigerate any unused chutney after defrosting.

Note: I never peel my ginger root before use. I wash it very well and then chop or grate it, peel and all, for use in recipes. I store leftover pieces of ginger immersed in dry sherry in a glass jar in the refrigerator. Not only does this preserve the fresh ginger, it imparts a wonderful flavor to the dry sherry. Use this ginger-infused sherry in marinades, salad dressings, or stir frys.

SZECHWAN CHICKEN SALAD
WITH CHOW MEIN NOODLES

This salad is a prime example of the culinary possibilities at your fingertips when you keep a well-stocked pantry. For an interesting variation, substitute cubes of pork or peeled shrimp for the chicken. (The shrimp will cook in a fraction of the time.)

SERVES 4

¼ cup soy sauce

2 tablespoons dark Asian sesame oil

2 tablespoons honey

2 tablespoons dry sherry

1 tablespoon chopped fresh ginger

3 green onions, chopped

1 tablespoon chile garlic paste

4 boneless, skinless chicken breasts

1 cup pineapple or orange juice

3 cups thinly sliced red cabbage

3 cups thinly sliced bok choy

2 carrots, shredded

1 red bell pepper, seeded and cut into thin matchsticks

1 cucumber, halved lengthwise, seeded, and cut
   into thin crescents

1 (8 ounce) can sliced water chestnuts, rinsed and drained

1 cup pineapple chunks (optional)

1 cup fresh bean sprouts

⅓ cup chopped fresh cilantro

¼ cup sesame seeds, lightly toasted (see page 9)

4 green onions, chopped

2 cups crunchy chow mein noodles

In a large bowl combine the soy sauce, dark Asian sesame oil, honey, sherry, ginger, green onions, and chile garlic paste. Add the chicken breasts and turn to coat evenly. Cover and refrigerate for 2 hours or overnight.

Preheat the oven to 425°F . Remove the chicken breasts from the marinade and return remaining marinade to the refrigerator. On a foil-lined baking sheet place the chicken breasts in a single layer. Cook for 18 to 22 minutes, turning once after 10 minutes. Remove the chicken breasts from the oven and cut into bite-sized pieces. Set aside.

Place the pineapple or orange juice and the reserved marinade in a 2-quart saucepan, bring to a boil, reduce the heat to a simmer, and cook, uncovered, for 10 minutes, skimming any foam or scum that rises to the top. Keep marinade warm.

In a large bowl combine the red cabbage, bok choy, carrots, red bell pepper, cucumber, water chestnuts, pineapple chunks, bean sprouts, and cilantro. Add chicken pieces, pour the warm marinade over the salad, and toss well. Sprinkle with toasted sesame seeds, green onions, and chow mein noodles. Toss once more. Serve warm or at room temperature.

CRUNCHY FRIED GREEN TOMATO SALAD WITH BACON VINAIGRETTE

Green tomatoes, which are simply unripened tomatoes, are easy to find in most large grocery stores or farm stands today. Be aware, if you buy them a few days ahead they will begin to ripen. To slow down this process, store them in a paper bag in your refrigerator's crisper drawer.

SERVES 4

10 slices of bacon, chopped

1 cup all-purpose flour

1 cup yellow cornmeal (not cornmeal mix)

1 teaspoon salt

½ teaspoon black pepper

4 green tomatoes, cored and sliced in ½-inch thick slices

About ½ cup peanut oil

1 garlic clove, chopped

½ cup apple cider vinegar

2 teaspoons Dijon mustard

⅓ cup olive oil

½ teaspoon sugar

10 cups mesclun

1 Vidalia onion, thinly sliced

1 very ripe tomato, seeded and finely diced

In a 10-inch skillet, preferably cast iron, fry the bacon over medium-high heat until golden brown. Remove the bacon with a slotted spoon and place on paper towels to drain. Measure out and set aside ½ cup of the drippings, leaving the remaining drippings in the skillet.

In a pie plate or shallow bowl combine the flour, cornmeal, salt, and pepper. Coat each tomato slice on both sides with the seasoned flour and place on a wire rack. Reserve the flour. Add ¼ cup of peanut oil to the skillet with the reserved drippings and heat over medium-high heat. Dredge the tomatoes in the seasoned flour again, then add them in batches to the hot skillet. Cook the tomatoes over medium-high heat, about 1 minute per side. Drain on paper towels. Repeat with the remaining slices until all of the tomatoes have been fried, adding more peanut oil as needed.

Make the bacon vinaigrette: In a small bowl whisk together the garlic, apple cider vinegar, Dijon mustard, and the ¼ cup reserved bacon drippings. Slowly whisk in the olive oil in a thin, steady stream until the dressing is thick and emulsified. Stir in the sugar and season to taste with salt and pepper.

Divide the mesclun among 4 individual serving plates. Top with the Vidalia onion and fried green tomatoes. Drizzle with the vinaigrette and garnish with the diced tomato and crispy fried bacon bits.

FRISÉE SALAD WITH PEARS & WALNUT-CRUSTED GOAT CHEESE ROUNDS

This salad may seem a bit complicated but, with a bit of organization, it comes together very easily. The goat cheese rounds can be coated and frozen several days in advance, and the dressing and Stilton butter keep well for 3 to 4 days in the refrigerator.

SERVES 4

1 (12 ounce) log goat cheese, such as Montrachet,
   very well chilled

1½ cups very finely chopped walnuts

2 teaspoons coarse-grained Dijon mustard

¼ cup champagne vinegar

½ cup sour cream

¼ cup extra-virgin olive oil

Salt and freshly ground black pepper

½ teaspoon sugar, or to taste

2 tablespoons chopped fresh chives

8 slices of bacon, chopped

1 head frisée (curly endive)

1 bunch watercress, stems removed

1 bunch arugula, stems removed

2 Belgian endive, thinly shaved

2 shallots, chopped

2 ripe Bosc pears, cored and thinly sliced lengthwise

Stilton Croûtes (recipe follows)

Preheat the oven to 350°F. Slice the goat cheese log into 12 rounds. Place the walnuts on a shallow plate. Roll the rounds of cheese into the walnuts, pressing so the nuts adhere to the cheese. Place the coated cheese rounds on a baking sheet lined with parchment paper. Cover and place in the freezer for 30 to 45 minutes.

In a small bowl whisk together the mustard, champagne vinegar, sour cream, and olive oil until the mixture is thick and emulsified. Season to taste with salt, pepper, and sugar. Stir in the chopped chives.

In a 10-inch skillet over medium-high heat, fry the bacon until crisp, 3 to 4 minutes. Remove the bacon with a slotted spoon and drain on paper towels.

Remove the cheese from the freezer and place in the preheated oven. Bake for 8 to 10 minutes, or until the rounds still hold their shape but are creamy when pierced with a knife.

In a large mixing bowl toss together the frisée, watercress, arugula, and Belgian endive. Divide among 4 serving plates. Top the greens with the shallots and pears. Arrange 3 baked goat cheese rounds on each plate. Drizzle the salad with the dressing and top with the crisped bacon. Serve at once with Stilton Croûtes.

STILTON CROÛTES

2 tablespoons butter, softened
1 (3 ounce) package cream cheese, softened
½ cup crumbled Stilton cheese
2 tablespoons chopped fresh chives
Salt and freshly ground black pepper
16 (¼-inch-thick) French baguette slices

Preheat the broiler. In a food processor combine the softened butter, cream cheese, Stilton cheese, chives, and salt and pepper to taste. Spread about 1 tablespoon of the Stilton butter onto each baguette slice. Arrange slices on a baking sheet and broil croûtes about 8 inches from the heat source for about 2 minutes, or until the cheese is bubbly. Serve hot or at room temperature.

DEVILISH EGG SALAD WITH SPINACH & BACON

For variety you can add 12 ounces of tuna fish, lump crab meat, or baby shrimp to the basic recipe. Or try the variation (see below), stuffing the eggs and serving as a side dish with fried chicken or a delicious hors d'oeuvre with smoked salmon.

SERVES 4

12 hard-cooked eggs, peeled and coarsely chopped (see note)

1 (6½ ounce) jar pasteurized cheese spread with olives or pimentos

1 (10 ounce) package frozen chopped spinach, defrosted and squeezed dry

8 slices of bacon, chopped, fried crisp, and drained

¼ cup mayonnaise

1 jalapeño pepper, seeded and chopped

4 green onions, chopped

1 teaspoon poultry seasoning

½ teaspoon celery seed

Salt and freshly ground black pepper

8 cups mesclun

1 tablespoon olive oil

1 tablespoon sherry vinegar

2 Belgian endive, separated into individual spears

Paprika

½ cup alfalfa sprouts (optional)

In a medium bowl combine the chopped eggs, cheese spread, spinach, bacon, mayonnaise, jalapeño pepper, green onions, poultry seasoning, celery seed, and salt and pepper to taste.

In a large bowl toss together the mesclun with the olive oil and sherry vinegar. Divide the mesclun among 4 individual salad plates. Mound the egg salad in the center of the lettuce. Arrange the endive spears decoratively around the egg salad so that the finished dish resembles a flower. Sprinkle with paprika and garnish with alfalfa sprouts, if desired.

Note: To hard cook eggs, place in a saucepan with enough water to cover by 2 inches. Add 1 tablespoon of distilled vinegar. Bring to a boil, remove from the heat, cover, and let sit for 16 to 18 minutes. Drain and rinse, then immerse the eggs in cold water for 1 to 2 minutes. Roll the eggs on the countertop to crack and peel under a thin stream of cold running water. Pat dry and refrigerate until ready to use.

Variation: Peel the eggs and cut in half lengthwise, discarding any that did not cook all the way through or are shaped unevenly. Place the yolks in a medium bowl and mash. Stir in the cheese spread, spinach, bacon, mayonnaise, jalapeño pepper, green onions, poultry seasoning, celery seed, and salt and pepper to taste. Refill each egg white with the egg yolk mixture, using about 1 tablespoon per half. Cover loosely and refrigerate for 3 hours or overnight. Sprinkle with paprika just before serving.

33

BROILED TUNA SALAD WITH ROASTED RED BELL PEPPER SAUCE

For a spectacular pasta salad variation, omit the mesclun and substitute 1 pound of cooked penne pasta. Toss everything together in one large bowl and sprinkle with grated Romano or Asiago cheese.

SERVES 4

1 cup chicken stock

3 roasted red bell peppers, peeled, seeded, and coarsely chopped

4 garlic cloves, chopped, divided

2 leeks, white and light green part only, cleaned and finely chopped

1 tablespoon freshly squeezed lemon juice

1 teaspoon sugar

¼ cup sherry vinegar

2 tablespoons chopped fresh parsley

Salt and freshly ground black pepper

4 (6 ounce) tuna steaks

½ cup freshly squeezed lime juice

Grated zest of 3 limes

2 tablespoons olive oil

4 green onions, chopped

½ cup honey

½ teaspoon red pepper flakes

1 red onion, chopped

2 fennel bulbs, cored and chopped

3 hard-cooked eggs, chopped (see page 33)

¼ cup chopped fresh dill

8 cups mesclun

In a 2-quart saucepan set over medium-high heat bring the chicken stock to a boil. Add the roasted red peppers, half of the chopped garlic, leeks, lemon juice, and sugar. Reduce the heat to medium and cook, uncovered, for 15 minutes. Pour the vegetables and stock into a food processor. Purée until smooth. Stir in the sherry vinegar and parsley. Season to taste with salt and pepper and set aside.

Preheat the broiler. Place the tuna steaks in a shallow non-reactive baking dish. In a small bowl whisk together the lime juice, lime zest, the remaining garlic, olive oil, green onions, honey, and red pepper flakes. Pour the marinade over the tuna steaks. Marinate at room temperature, uncovered, for 30 minutes, turning the steaks after 15 minutes. Place the tuna steaks on a foil-lined baking sheet and broil for 3 to 4 minutes per side, turning once. Remove from the oven and cut into ¾-inch pieces.

Combine the tuna with the red onion, fennel, hard-cooked eggs, and dill. Divide the mesclun among 4 individual serving plates. Mound the tuna mixture in the center of the lettuce and spoon the red bell pepper sauce over the tuna.

ITALIAN SEAFOOD SALAD

If you want, add crab meat, chunks of cooked lobster tail, or calamari to this innovative dish.

1 pound medium shrimp, peeled and deveined

1 pound sea scallops, rinsed and drained

½ cup peanut oil

6 garlic cloves, chopped

⅔ cup chopped flatleaf (Italian) parsley, divided

Grated zest of 2 lemons

¼ cup freshly squeezed lemon juice

1 teaspoon Dijon mustard

¼ cup olive oil

1 teaspoon sugar

½ teaspoon salt

½ teaspoon black pepper

6 green onions, chopped

2 ribs of celery, thinly sliced

2 fennel bulbs, cored and thinly sliced

2 roasted red bell peppers, peeled, seeded, and thinly sliced

4 large romaine lettuce leaves

½ cup pine nuts, lightly toasted (see page 9)

½ cup grated Parmesan cheese

Six hours ahead or the night before: Season the shrimp and scallops lightly with salt and pepper. In a 10-inch skillet set over medium-high heat, heat the peanut oil until hot, add the garlic and half of the chopped parsley, reduce the heat to medium, and cook for 1 minute. Add the shrimp and sauté until the shrimp turn pink and begin to curl, about 3 minutes. Remove the shrimp with a slotted spoon and place in a large bowl. Add the lemon zest to the hot oil, then add the scallops. Cook, stirring frequently, until the scallops become firm and opaque, about 3 minutes. Remove with a slotted spoon and place in the bowl with the shrimp.

In a small bowl, whisk together the lemon juice, Dijon mustard, olive oil, sugar, salt, and pepper. Pour over the cooked seafood and toss to coat. Add the green onions, celery, fennel, and roasted pepper slices. Toss to coat completely. Cover and refrigerate at least 6 hours, or overnight.

Place 1 large romaine leaf on each of 4 individual serving plates. Spoon the seafood and vegetables over the lettuce. Sprinkle with pine nuts, Parmesan cheese, and remaining parsley. Serve at once.

CARIBBEAN SHRIMP SALAD WITH CANTALOUPE MANGO SALSA

The salsa in this salad is also delicious served with smoked chicken, honey-crusted ham steaks, or grilled salmon. It makes a delightful change from tomato-based salsas when served with crispy corn tortilla chips.

SERVES 4

½ cantaloupe, peeled and cut into ½-inch dice

2 mangos, peeled and cut into ½-inch dice

1 small red onion, finely chopped

1 tablespoon chopped fresh ginger

½ cup chopped walnuts, lightly toasted (see page 9)

2 tablespoons freshly squeezed lime juice

1 tablespoon soy sauce

1 tablespoon dark Asian sesame oil

⅓ cup chopped fresh cilantro

1 or 2 jalapeño peppers, seeded and finely chopped

2 pounds large shrimp, peeled and deveined

¼ cup olive oil

3 garlic cloves, chopped

2 tablespoons chopped fresh parsley

¼ teaspoon red pepper flakes

Juice of 2 oranges

Zest of 3 oranges

8 cups bite-sized pieces of Boston lettuce

2 cups thinly sliced radicchio

Several hours before serving: In a medium bowl toss together the cantaloupe, mango, onion, ginger, walnuts, lime juice, soy sauce, sesame oil, cilantro, and jalapeño peppers. Taste and add salt and pepper accordingly. Cover and refrigerate for at least 4 hours or up to 3 days. One hour before serving, remove from refrigerator and let sit at room temperature.

Spread the shrimp out on a paper towel and blot dry with another towel. Season lightly with salt and pepper.

In a 12-inch skillet or sauté pan heat the olive oil over medium-high heat until hot. Add the garlic, parsley, and red pepper flakes. Cook, stirring constantly, for 30 seconds. Add the shrimp and quickly sauté, until the shrimp begin to curl and turn pink, 2 to 3 minutes. Add the orange juice and zest, cover, and allow the shrimp to steam for about 1 minute more. Remove from heat.

In a large bowl toss together the Boston lettuce and radicchio. Divide among 4 individual serving plates. Spoon the shrimp and the orange-flavored cooking broth over the salad greens. Mound the salsa in the center of the plates. Serve immediately.

Note: Be sure not to overcook the shrimp, as they will become tough and rubbery. A perfectly cooked shrimp should be a vibrant coral pink and form the letter "C". If the tail curls too much and almost touches the other end, the shrimp is overcooked.

PICKLED CUCUMBER CRESCENTS
& CRAB SALAD

This salad is even better when made a day ahead and allowed to marinate overnight. I've used some distinctly Asian overtones in the flavoring. If you want to vary this, omit the rice wine vinegar, sesame oil, fish sauce, and cilantro and substitute ½ cup apple cider vinegar, 1 tablespoon Dijon mustard, 1 tablespoon Worcestershire sauce, and ¼ cup chopped fresh basil.

SERVES 4

*1 large English cucumber, cut in half lengthwise and
   thinly sliced on the diagonal*

1 red onion, thinly sliced

2 green bell peppers, seeded and thinly sliced

1 cup quartered cherry tomatoes

1½ pounds lump crabmeat, picked over

4 green onions, chopped

½ cup rice wine vinegar

½ cup peanut oil

1 tablespoon dark Asian sesame oil

2 tablespoons fish sauce

¼ cup chopped fresh cilantro

1 teaspoon celery seeds

1 tablespoon sugar

½ teaspoon salt

½ teaspoon black pepper

¼ teaspoon red pepper flakes

⅓ cup lightly toasted sesame seeds (see page 9)

Whole Bibb lettuce leaves

½ cup chopped dry-roasted peanuts

Several hours ahead or the night before: In a large bowl toss together the cucumber, red onion, green bell peppers, cherry tomatoes, crabmeat, and green onions. In a small bowl whisk together the rice wine vinegar, peanut oil, sesame oil, fish sauce, cilantro, celery seeds, sugar, salt, black pepper, red pepper flakes, and sesame seeds.

Pour the vinaigrette over the salad, cover, and marinate in the refrigerator for several hours or overnight. Line a serving platter with Bibb lettuce leaves. Mound the crab salad in the center. Sprinkle with the chopped peanuts and serve at once.

POACHED SALMON AND SOUR CREAM POTATO SALAD WITH SALMON ROE

This salad is perfect for a Mother's Day dinner, a spring luncheon, or a Sunday brunch.

SERVES 4

12 red new potatoes, scrubbed

2 tablespoons white wine vinegar

⅓ cup chopped fresh dill

1 tablespoon chopped fresh tarragon

Salt and freshly ground black pepper

1 pound asparagus, woody stems removed

1 red onion, chopped

1 red bell pepper, seeded and chopped

3 green onions, chopped

1 rib of celery, thinly sliced

2 hard-cooked eggs, chopped (see page 33)

1½ cups sour cream, divided

⅓ cup mayonnaise

2 tablespoons freshly squeezed lemon juice

⅔ cup crumbled feta cheese

1 teaspoon sugar

1 small yellow onion, sliced

4 parsley stalks

1 lemon, sliced

10 black peppercorns

4 (6 ounce) boneless, skinless salmon fillets

¼ cup salmon roe

1 lemon, cut into 8 wedges

1 tablespoon paprika

Place the potatoes in a 2½-quart saucepan with enough lightly salted water to cover them by 2 inches. Bring to a boil and cook, uncovered, for 10 to 12 minutes, or until tender. Remove and refresh under cold running water. Cover the saucepan and keep the cooking water at a simmer. When the potatoes are cool, thinly slice and place in a large bowl. Stir in the white wine vinegar, dill, and tarragon. Gently toss and season with salt and pepper. Add the asparagus to the simmering water and cook for 2 to 3 minutes, or until crisp-tender. Drain and season to taste with salt and pepper.

In a large bowl mix together the new potatoes, red onion, red bell pepper, green onions, celery, and egg. In a small bowl combine 1 cup of the sour cream with the mayonnaise, lemon juice, feta cheese, and sugar. Toss the potatoes with the dressing.

Poach the salmon: In a deep 10-inch skillet combine the yellow onion slices, parsley stalks, lemon slices, and peppercorns. Add enough water to cover the vegetables by 2 inches. Bring to a boil, reduce the heat to a simmer, and with a slotted spoon carefully lower the salmon fillets into the simmering water. Cover and cook until the salmon flakes easily with a fork, about 10 minutes per inch of thickness. Remove and drain on paper towels.

Divide the potato salad among 4 individual serving plates. Arrange the asparagus on each side of the potato salad. Drape a salmon fillet over each salad. Dollop each fillet with 2 tablespoons of the remaining sour cream. Place the salmon roe on top of the sour cream. Garnish with lemon wedges dipped in paprika. Serve at once.

PROSCIUTTO-WRAPPED FIGS ON ARUGULA & FRESH HERB BED

I am fortunate enough to have a couple of fig trees growing in my back yard. Those that I don't share with the birds
(not voluntarily) get made into preserves or chutney; used as a filling for cakes, pies, and cookies
(home-made fig Newtons are the best); or enjoyed whole in this salad.

SERVES 4

16 fresh large black mission figs

16 thin slices prosciutto ham

2 cups cantaloupe balls

2 cups honeydew melon balls

2 tablespoons honey

Juice of 3 limes

Grated zest of 2 limes

¼ cup champagne or white wine vinegar

¼ cup hazelnut oil

½ cup extra-virgin olive oil

1 teaspoon salt

1 tablespoon pink peppercorns, crushed

4 cups arugula leaves, stems removed

2 cups frisée, torn into bite-sized pieces

1 cup basil leaves

½ cup mint leaves

¼ cup chopped fresh chervil

1 cup shaved Parmesan cheese

1 cup lightly toasted hazelnuts, skins rubbed off (see note)

Pesticide-free rose petals for garnish (about 1 rose), optional

Cut the figs into quarters but do not cut all the way through to the ends. Fold the slices of prosciutto in half lengthwise, then wrap around the base of the figs, forming a ruffled rim around the bottom of each fig. In a medium bowl toss together the cantaloupe and honeydew melon balls.

In a small bowl combine the honey, lime juice, lime zest, vinegar, hazelnut oil, olive oil, salt, and crushed peppercorns. Whisk well to thoroughly combine.

In a large bowl combine the arugula, frisée, basil, mint, and chervil. Divide the greens among 4 individual serving plates. Nestle 4 figs into the greens on each plate. Spoon the melon balls around each salad. Drizzle each salad with the dressing. Top with shaved Parmesan and hazelnuts. Garnish with rose petals, if desired.

Variation: The figs can be wrapped with thin slices of bacon or pancetta and grilled or broiled 5 to 7 minutes, or until the slices are golden brown. Drain on paper towels before nesting the figs in the salad.

Note: After toasting the hazelnuts (see page 9), place them on one half of a tea towel. Fold the other half of the towel over the nuts and rub back and forth with your hands. The skins should slip right off.

SPICED CHOPPED HAM
& PINEAPPLE SALAD WITH
RASPBERRY VINAIGRETTE

This salad reminds me of the baked ham, glazed with brown sugar, topped with pineapple rings, and studded with fresh cloves, that was a springtime family favorite. This easy, vibrantly colored salad would make a wonderful choice for Easter brunch.

SERVES 4

⅓ cup raspberry vinegar

1 teaspoon Dijon mustard

1 tablespoon sugar

½ teaspoon salt

½ teaspoon black pepper

1 tablespoon poppy seeds

⅛ teaspoon ground cloves

½ cup extra-virgin olive oil

1½ pounds very coarsely chopped baked ham

6 cups mesclun

2 cups pineapple chunks

1 red onion, thinly sliced

1 cup sliced mushrooms

2 ripe avocados, halved, peeled, and pitted

2 tablespoons freshly squeezed lemon juice

1 cup sliced almonds, lightly toasted (see page 9)

1 cup fresh raspberries

In a small bowl whisk together the raspberry vinegar, Dijon mustard, sugar, salt, pepper, poppy seeds, and ground cloves. Add the olive oil in a thin, steady stream, whisking constantly until the dressing is thick and emulsified. Set aside.

In a large bowl toss together the chopped ham, mesclun, pineapple chunks, red onion, and mushrooms. Pour half of the dressing on the salad and toss to coat. Divide the salad among 4 individual serving plates. Thinly slice the avocado and toss with the lemon juice to prevent the avocado from darkening. Place the avocado on top of the salad and sprinkle with toasted almonds and raspberries. Drizzle the remaining dressing on the salad and serve at once.

41

SALAD SUPPERS

Turkey and Roasted Sweet Potato Salad with Cranberry Sage Vinaigrette

Oven-Roasted Root Vegetable Salad with Creamy Herb Dressing

Crispy Fried Catfish and Cabbage Salad with Tangy Buttermilk Dressing

Fried Chicken Salad with Peach and Honey Mustard Dressing

Fiesta Taco Salad with Salsa Dressing

White Bean Salad with Baby Shrimp and Tarragon Vinaigrette

Smoked Trout and Apple Salad with Spicy Pecan Vinaigrette

Fajita Beef and Jicama Salad with Jalepeño Vinaigrette

Farfalle and Red Bell Pepper Salad with Parmesan Vinaigrette

Beef au Poivre and Apple Salad with Gorgonzola Cheese Dressing

TURKEY & ROASTED SWEET POTATO SALAD WITH CRANBERRY SAGE VINAIGRETTE

This salad is an excellent way to disguise holiday leftovers, but it is also delicious served anytime throughout the year.

SERVES 4

3 sweet potatoes, peeled and cut into ½-inch dice

2 tablespoons olive oil

Salt and freshly ground black pepper

3 cups shredded cooked turkey or chicken

1 red onion, chopped

2 ribs of celery, thinly sliced

2 Golden Delicious apples, cored and cut into bite-sized chunks

1 cup chopped pecans, toasted (see page 9)

¼ cup chopped fresh parsley

2 cups Seasoned Croutons (recipe follows)

⅓ cup raspberry vinegar

1 tablespoon Dijon mustard

2 tablespoons honey

½ cup prepared whole-berry cranberry sauce

½ cup extra-virgin olive oil

1 tablespoon chopped fresh sage

1 teaspoon poultry seasoning

¼ cup sour cream

8 cups mesclun

Preheat the oven to 350°F. Line a 15 x 10 x 1-inch baking sheet with aluminum foil. In a medium bowl toss the cubed sweet potatoes with the olive oil. Season lightly with salt and pepper. Place the sweet potatoes on the baking sheet. Bake for 35 to 45 minutes, or until the potatoes begin to brown on the outside and are tender when pierced with a fork.

Transfer the potatoes to a large bowl. Add the turkey, red onion, celery, apples, pecans, parsley, and croutons. Season to taste with salt and pepper.

Make the cranberry sage vinaigrette: In a food processor combine the raspberry vinegar, Dijon mustard, honey, cranberry sauce, ½ teaspoon of salt, and ½ teaspoon of black pepper. Process until smooth. With the machine running, slowly add the olive oil in a thin, steady stream until the vinaigrette is thick and emulsified. Remove to a medium bowl and whisk in the sage, poultry seasoning, and sour cream. Taste and adjust seasonings with additional salt and pepper as desired.

Divide the mesclun among 4 serving plates and top with the turkey mixture. Drizzle with the vinaigrette. Serve at once.

SEASONED CROUTONS

8 thick slices day-old French bread, cubed
1 tablespoon dried Italian seasoning
½ teaspoon onion powder
½ teaspoon garlic powder
¼ teaspoon cayenne pepper
⅓ cup freshly grated Parmesan cheese
⅓ cup olive oil

Preheat the oven to 350°F. In a large bowl combine the cubed bread with the Italian seasoning, onion powder, garlic powder, cayenne pepper, and Parmesan cheese. Drizzle with the olive oil and toss well to coat completely. Spread the bread cubes on a large baking sheet. Bake for 10 to 15 minutes, or until golden and crisp, stirring occasionally. Store in an airtight container for up to 1 week or freeze for up to 1 month.

OVEN-ROASTED ROOT VEGETABLE SALAD WITH CREAMY HERB DRESSING

The vegetables take on a whole new dimension of flavor when allowed to crisp and caramelize in the oven. I enjoy this as a vegetarian entrée, but slices of rare-roasted beef or lamb make a nice addition.

SERVES 4

8 shallots, peeled and halved

16 garlic cloves, peeled

2 sweet potatoes, peeled and cut into ¾-inch dice

6 small new potatoes, scrubbed and quartered

2 carrots, peeled and cut into ¾-inch chunks

2 parsnips, peeled and cut into ¾-inch chunks

2 turnips, peeled and cut into ¾-inch chunks

¼ cup peanut oil

2 tablespoons chopped fresh rosemary

Salt and freshly ground black pepper

1 cup plain yogurt or sour cream

¼ cup mayonnaise

1 tablespoon coarse-grained Dijon mustard

Juice of 1 lemon

1 cup assorted chopped fresh herbs (such as parsley, tarragon, chervil, and chives)

1 (15½ ounce) can sliced beets, drained, each slice cut in half

2 hard-cooked eggs, peeled and coarsely chopped

2 green onions, chopped

Preheat the oven to 400°F. Line a 15 x 10 x 1-inch baking sheet with heavy-duty aluminum foil. In a large bowl combine the shallots, garlic, sweet potatoes, new potatoes, carrots, parsnips, and turnips. Drizzle with the peanut oil and sprinkle with the rosemary and salt and pepper to taste. Toss to coat completely. Roast for 1 to 1¼ hours, stirring every 15 minutes, until the vegetables are browned on the outside and tender when pierced with a fork. Set aside to cool. Transfer vegetables to a large bowl.

Make the creamy herb dressing: In a small bowl whisk together the yogurt or sour cream, mayonnaise, mustard, lemon juice, fresh herbs, ½ teaspoon salt, and ½ teaspoon black pepper. Add dressing to the roasted vegetables and toss to coat.

Mound the vegetables on a large platter and place the beet halves around the circumference of the salad. Sprinkle with the chopped egg and green onions. Serve warm or at room temperature.

CRISPY FRIED CATFISH & CABBAGE SALAD WITH TANGY BUTTERMILK DRESSING

This recipe was so popular when I tested it that it became the featured selection at an impromptu neighborhood block party. Tilapia, flounder, red snapper, or cod all work well if catfish is unavailable.

SERVES 4

1 cup plain yogurt

½ cup mayonnaise

1¼ cups buttermilk, divided

2 teaspoons Dijon mustard

2 tablespoons freshly squeezed lemon juice

¼ cup apple cider vinegar

2 tablespoons chopped fresh chives

1 teaspoon onion powder

½ teaspoon garlic powder

½ teaspoon celery seeds

Salt and freshly ground black pepper

3 cups thinly sliced red cabbage

3 cups thinly sliced green cabbage

1 carrot, shredded

1 red onion, thinly sliced

1 Granny Smith apple, cored and cut into small chunks

1 Bosc pear, cored and cut into small chunks

1 cup seedless red grapes, halved

⅔ cup golden raisins

⅔ cup sliced almonds, lightly toasted (see page 9)

8 (4 to 6 ounce) catfish fillets

2 eggs

1 teaspoon Tabasco

2 cups yellow cornmeal (not cornmeal mix)

Peanut oil for frying

Make the dressing: In a small bowl whisk together the yogurt, mayonnaise, ½ cup of the buttermilk, Dijon mustard, lemon juice, apple cider vinegar, chives, onion powder, garlic powder, celery seeds, and salt and pepper to taste.

In a large bowl combine the red and green cabbage, carrot, red onion, apple, pear, grapes, raisins, and almonds. Pour half of the dressing over the salad and toss to coat. Reserve the remaining dressing.

Rinse the catfish fillets and pat dry with a paper towel. In a shallow bowl whisk together the remaining cup of buttermilk, eggs and Tabasco. In a separate shallow bowl combine the cornmeal, with ½ teaspoon of salt and 1 teaspoon of black pepper. Dip each fillet into the buttermilk, then dredge in the cornmeal mixture. Shake off any excess. Repeat with remaining fillets.

Pour about 1 inch of peanut oil into a 12-inch heavy skillet. Heat the oil to a temperature of about 360°F. Fry the fillets until they are golden brown on both sides, about 3 to 4 minutes per side. Be sure to regulate the heat of the oil. If it is too hot, the fish will burn. If it is not hot enough, the fish will have a greasy, soggy texture. Drain on paper towels.

Divide the salad among 4 individual serving plates. Top each salad with 2 catfish fillets and drizzle with the remaining dressing.

FRIED CHICKEN SALAD WITH PEACH & HONEY MUSTARD DRESSING

If you do not have a kitchen thermometer to test the temperature of the oil, follow this guideline: A cube of bread will fry golden and crisp in about 45 seconds when the oil has reached the correct temperature. It is very important to maintain the correct frying temperature. If the heat of the oil is too high, the chicken will burn on the outside before it is cooked through in the center. If it is too low, the chicken will become greasy.

SERVES 4

1 cup shortening, melted, or vegetable oil

1 cup buttermilk

½ teaspoon Tabasco

2 cups all purpose flour

½ teaspoon salt

½ teaspoon black pepper

1 teaspoon poultry seasoning

1 teaspoon garlic powder

1 teaspoon onion powder

6 boneless, skinless chicken breasts, rinsed and patted dry, cut into 1-inch strips

8 cups frisée or curly endive, torn

1 Vidalia onion, thinly sliced

1 cup toasted pecan halves (see page 9)

1 cup crumbled blue cheese

Dressing

2 peaches, peeled, pitted, and cut into 1-inch cubes

1 tablespoon Dijon mustard

2 teaspoons dry mustard, such as Coleman's

2 garlic cloves, chopped

⅓ cup honey

⅓ cup apple cider vinegar

1 cup peanut oil or vegetable oil

1 teaspoon salt

2 teaspoons sugar

1 teaspoon black pepper

1 teaspoon celery seeds

In a 12-inch deep skillet or frying pan, heat the shortening or vegetable oil to 360°F.

While the shortening or oil is heating, in a small bowl combine the buttermilk and Tabasco. In a shallow pie plate or dish combine the flour, salt, pepper, poultry seasoning, garlic powder, and onion powder. Dip the chicken strips into the egg/buttermilk mixture, then dredge in the seasoned flour. Place on a wire rack. Place the chicken strips, in batches if necessary, in the hot oil. Allow the pieces to slightly touch but do not overcrowd the pan. Reduce the heat to medium-high and cook the chicken for 10 to 12 minutes, or until golden brown. Remove and drain on paper towels.

Make the dressing: In a food processor place the peaches, Dijon mustard, dry mustard, garlic, honey, and apple cider vinegar. With the machine running, slowly add the oil in a thin, steady stream until dressing is thick and emulsified. Add the salt, sugar, pepper, and celery seeds and process for 15 seconds. Taste for seasoning and add more according to your taste.

Place the chicken strips in a medium bowl. Add half of the dressing and toss to coat evenly. Let marinate at room temperature for at least 1 hour.

When ready to serve toss together the frisée and onion slices in a large bowl. Arrange the lettuce mixture on 4 individual serving plates. Divide the chicken strips among the plates. Top with the toasted pecans and blue cheese. Drizzle with the remaining dressing.

FIESTA TACO SALAD WITH SALSA DRESSING

I don't know of anyone — kids or grown-ups — who doesn't love this easy salad supper. If you want, serve this salad in the pre-made tortilla "bowls" found in the cheese section of your grocery store.

SERVES 4

1 pound lean ground beef

1 pound hot Italian pork sausage

6 green onions, chopped

3 garlic cloves, chopped

1 (15½ ounce) can kidney beans, rinsed and drained

1½ cups tomato sauce

1 (4 ounce) can chopped mild green chiles, drained

1 tablespoon chili powder

2 teaspoons ground cumin

2 teaspoons dried oregano

1½ cups sour cream

½ cup mild or medium-hot chunky salsa

1 (12 ounce) package taco seasoning mix

1 head iceberg lettuce, cored and thinly sliced

3 tomatoes, seeded and chopped

1 small red onion, chopped

1 cup grated cheddar cheese

1 cup grated Monterey Jack cheese

2 cups coarsely broken tortilla chips

1 (4 ounce) can sliced black olives, drained

In a deep 10-inch skillet over medium-high heat cook the ground beef, Italian sausage, green onions, and garlic for about 8 minutes, or until the meat is nicely browned, stirring to break up the meat. Drain excess fat from the skillet.

Add the kidney beans, tomato sauce, green chiles, chili powder, cumin, and oregano. Cook over medium heat, stirring frequently to mash the beans, for about 10 minutes, or until most of the liquid is absorbed. Set aside.

In a medium bowl whisk together the sour cream, salsa, and taco seasoning.

Divide the iceberg lettuce among 4 individual serving plates. Spoon the meat mixture on top of the lettuce. Scatter the tomatoes, red onion, cheddar cheese, and Monterey Jack cheese over the meat. Spoon the salsa dressing over the cheese. Top each salad with the broken tortilla chips and black olives. Serve at once.

WHITE BEAN SALAD WITH BABY SHRIMP & TARRAGON VINAIGRETTE

One of my all-time favorites, this luscious salad of mellow white beans, bacon, tarragon, and niçoise olives can be put together in minutes. You can even make it up to 2 days ahead and store it, tightly wrapped, in the refrigerator. For optimum flavor, let the salad come to room temperature before serving.

SERVES 4

6 slices of bacon, coarsely chopped

⅓ cup apple cider vinegar

2 tablespoons brown sugar

3 tablespoons chopped fresh tarragon

⅓ cup extra-virgin olive oil

Salt and freshly ground black pepper

2 (15½ ounce) cans white beans, rinsed and drained

1 pound frozen cooked baby shrimp (sometimes called "salad" shrimp), thawed

1 red onion, chopped

4 garlic cloves, chopped

2 ribs of celery, thinly sliced

2 carrots, shredded

4 plum tomatoes, seeded and coarsely chopped

1 small English cucumber, cut in half lengthwise, seeded, and finely diced

2 cups Seasoned Croutons (see page 45)

½ cup pitted niçoise olives

2 green onions, finely chopped

In a 12-inch skillet cook the bacon over medium-high heat until crispy and golden brown, about 5 minutes. Remove the bacon to paper towels to drain.

Reduce the heat to low and add the apple cider vinegar to the hot drippings, scraping to loosen any browned bits on the bottom of the pan. Remove from the heat and stir in the brown sugar and tarragon. Whisk in the olive oil and salt and pepper to taste. Set aside.

In a large bowl combine the white beans, shrimp, red onion, garlic, celery, carrots, tomatoes, cucumber, and croutons. Add the vinaigrette and toss to coat completely.

Transfer salad to a large serving platter and top with the reserved bacon, niçoise olives, and green onions. Serve at once.

SMOKED TROUT & APPLE SALAD WITH SPICY PECAN VINAIGRETTE

I like serving this savory salad any time of year, but I particularly remember enjoying it with friends on a crisp autumn day, by a crackling fire at a mountain retreat — truly heaven on earth.

SERVES 4

2 Granny Smith apples

¼ cup plus 1 tablespoon freshly squeezed lemon juice

2 (1 pound) smoked trout, deboned and skin removed

1 red onion, thinly sliced

1 red bell pepper, seeded and thinly sliced

1 green bell pepper, seeded and thinly sliced

1 yellow bell pepper, seeded and thinly sliced

¼ cup pepper-flavored vodka

1 tablespoon coarse-grained Dijon mustard

2 tablespoons prepared horseradish

2 garlic cloves, chopped

1 tablespoon capers, rinsed and drained

1 teaspoon Tabasco, or to taste

¾ cup extra-virgin olive oil

½ teaspoon salt

½ teaspoon black pepper

1 teaspoon sugar

⅔ cup chopped pecans, lightly toasted (see page 9)

2 tablespoons chopped parsley

Halve, core, and thinly slice the apples. Toss them with 1 tablespoon lemon juice to prevent them from turning dark. Pick through the smoked trout for any small bones. Flake the fish until it is broken up into bite-sized pieces. In a large bowl combine the smoked trout, red onion, red, green, and yellow bell peppers, and the apples.

Make the vinaigrette: In a small bowl mix together the pepper-flavored vodka, the remaining ¼ cup of lemon juice, mustard, horseradish, garlic, capers, and Tabasco. Whisk in the olive oil until mixture is thoroughly combined. Add the salt, pepper, sugar, and pecans. Taste and adjust seasonings with additional salt and pepper. Pour the vinaigrette over the salad and let sit at room temperature for 30 minutes.

Just before serving toss once more and sprinkle with chopped parsley.

FAJITA BEEF AND JICAMA SALAD WITH JALEPEÑO VINAIGRETTE

The sweetness from the navel oranges and dried cranberries balances the heat from the jalapeños in the vinaigrette. For a smoky tang, substitute 2 tablespoons chopped chipotles in adobo sauce for the jalapeños.

SERVES 4

1 pound flank steak, thinly sliced on the diagonal

Juice of 3 limes

6 garlic cloves, chopped

²⁄₃ cup chopped fresh cilantro, divided

1 jicama, peeled and cut into 2-inch matchsticks

1 red bell pepper, seeded and cut into 2-inch matchsticks

1 red onion, thinly sliced

2 navel oranges, peeled and thinly sliced

1 (15½ ounce) can pinto beans, rinsed and drained

1 cup dried cranberries

¼ cup raspberry vinegar

¼ cup freshly squeezed orange juice

1 tablespoon Dijon mustard

2 teaspoons cumin seed, crushed

1 tablespoon chili powder

½ teaspoon salt

½ teaspoon black pepper

1 teaspoon sugar

½ cup olive oil

1 jalapeño pepper, seeded and finely chopped

Cilantro sprigs for garnish

Preheat the broiler. In a shallow glass pan gently toss the sliced flank steak, lime juice, half of the chopped garlic and ¹⁄₃ cup of the chopped cilantro. Marinate at room temperature for 15 minutes.

In a large bowl combine the jicama, red bell pepper, red onion, navel orange slices, pinto beans, dried cranberries, and the remaining ¹⁄₃ cup of chopped cilantro.

Make the vinaigrette: In a small bowl combine the raspberry vinegar, orange juice, Dijon mustard, the remaining chopped garlic, crushed cumin seed, chili powder, salt, pepper, and sugar. Slowly whisk in the olive oil in a thin, steady stream. Stir in the jalapeño pepper.

Place the marinated flank steak on a large broiler pan that has been lightly coated with nonstick cooking spray. Broil, approximately 6 inches from the heat source, about 4 to 5 minutes, or until the meat is medium-rare.

Toss the cooked beef with the vegetables. Pour the vinaigrette over the salad and toss to coat. Let sit at room temperature at least 1 hour before serving. Adjust seasonings with additional salt and pepper if necessary. Garnish with fresh sprigs of cilantro.

FARFALLE & RED BELL PEPPER SALAD WITH PARMESAN VINAIGRETTE

This pasta salad develops a marvelous flavor from the reduction of the red wine with the sautéed vegetables.

SERVES 4

2 tablespoons butter

2 cups sliced shiitake mushrooms

1 red onion, thinly sliced

4 red bell peppers, seeded and thinly sliced

4 garlic cloves, chopped

1 cup red wine

1 (16 ounce) jar marinated artichoke hearts,
    drained and cut in thirds

12 ounces farfalle or other short-shaped pasta,
    cooked according to package directions and drained

8 ounces smoked mozzarella, cut into ½-inch cubes

1 cup tightly packed basil leaves

½ head radicchio, thinly sliced

⅓ cup balsamic vinegar

1 tablespoon Dijon mustard

1 shallot, chopped

⅔ cup extra-virgin olive oil

½ cup grated Parmesan cheese

1 tablespoon chopped fresh oregano

Salt and freshly ground black pepper

In a 12-inch skillet melt the butter over medium-high heat. Add the mushrooms and sauté until soft, about 5 minutes. Add the red onion, red bell pepper, and garlic. Cook for 2 minutes. Add the red wine, bring to a boil, and cook until the red wine has totally evaporated, 5 to 7 minutes.

In a large bowl toss the sautéed vegetables with the artichoke hearts, farfalle, smoked mozzarella, basil leaves, and radicchio.

In a small bowl whisk together the balsamic vinegar, Dijon mustard, shallot, olive oil, Parmesan cheese, oregano, and salt and pepper to taste. Pour the dressing over the pasta and toss well. Serve at once, or cover and refrigerate for 2 to 3 days, allowing the salad to come to room temperature before eating.

BEEF AU POIVRE & APPLE SALAD WITH GORGONZOLA CHEESE DRESSING

You can substitute leftover cooked tenderloin or roast beef or strips of baked ham for the sirloin or London broil. The apples and fennel provide a wonderful crunch contrast and nicely balance the flavor of the robust dressing.

SERVES 4

A (2 pound) sirloin steak or London broil

3 tablespoons freshly cracked black pepper

2 Granny Smith apples, halved, cored, and thinly sliced

2 fennel bulbs, cored and thinly sliced

1 cup thinly sliced radishes

2 tablespoons freshly squeezed lemon juice

1 cup sour cream

¼ cup mayonnaise

2 garlic cloves, chopped

1 tablespoon Worcestershire sauce

1 tablespoon prepared horseradish

4 ounces Gorgonzola cheese, crumbled (about 1 cup), divided

4 green onions, chopped

2 tablespoons capers, rinsed and drained

Salt and freshly ground black pepper

6 cups mesclun

2 Belgian endive, cored and thinly sliced

¼ cup chopped fresh basil

Preheat the broiler. Rub the steak on both sides with the cracked pepper. Place under the broiler, about 6 inches from the heat source, and broil for about 4 minutes per side, turning once, for medium-rare meat. Remove from the oven and allow the steak to sit for 15 minutes. Slice steak into thin slices on the diagonal.

In a large bowl toss together the apples, fennel, radishes, and lemon juice. Add the beef to the apple mixture. Set aside.

Make the dressing: In a food processor combine the sour cream, mayonnaise, garlic, Worcestershire sauce, horseradish, and half of the Gorgonzola. Process until smooth. Transfer to a small bowl and add the green onions, capers, and remaining Gorgonzola. Season to taste with salt and pepper.

In a large bowl toss together the mesclun and Belgian endive. Divide the lettuce among 4 individual serving plates. Mound the beef and apple mixture in the center of the plates and spoon the dressing liberally over the salads. Garnish with chopped basil. Serve at once.

NEW CLASSIC SALADS

Turkey Paella Salad

Baba Ghanoush Salad (Roasted Eggplant Salad)

Classic Caesar Salad with International Variations

Italian Cobb Salad

Tandoori-Style Chicken Salad with Raita Cucumber Dressing

Philly Cheese Steak Salad with Peppercorn Dressing

Cod Salad Niçoise

Sautéed Ratatouille Salad with Minute Beef Steaks

Sesame and Ginger Vegetable and Garlic Beef Salad

Asian Cabbage Salad with Stir-fried Pork and Peanuts

Jack Cheese Quesadilla Salad with Cilantro Lime Vinaigrette

Warm German Potato Salad with Sausages and Caraway Vinaigrette

TURKEY PAELLA SALAD

This salad tastes like a traditional Spanish paella but is much easier to put together and can be made with leftover rice, turkey, and ham. I often freeze my leftover rice just to have on hand for this dish. Experiment and add cooked shrimp, salmon, cod, or other seafood.

SERVES 4

¼ cup freshly squeezed lemon juice

½ teaspoon saffron threads

1 teaspoon paprika

2 teaspoons Dijon mustard

2 garlic cloves, chopped

½ cup extra-virgin olive oil

Salt and freshly ground black pepper

½ teaspoon sugar

2 tablespoons chopped parsley

6 strips of bacon, chopped, or 2 tablespoons vegetable oil

1 onion, thinly sliced

1 cup frozen green peas, thawed

2 carrots, shredded

1 red bell pepper, seeded and chopped

4 plum tomatoes, seeded and coarsely chopped

¼ cup chopped fresh basil

4 cups cooked white rice

2 cups chopped cooked turkey

1 cup diced cooked ham

1 head romaine lettuce, separated into leaves

4 green onions, chopped

Make the vinaigrette: In a medium bowl mix together the lemon juice and saffron threads. Let sit for 10 minutes. Add the paprika, Dijon mustard, garlic, olive oil, salt and pepper to taste, and sugar. Whisk until thoroughly combined. Stir in the parsley and set aside.

In a 12-inch deep skillet or sauté pan over medium-high heat, fry the bacon until golden and crisp. Remove the bacon with a slotted spoon and drain on paper towels. Return the skillet with the drippings to the heat. (If using vegetable oil instead of bacon drippings, heat the oil in the skillet at this point.) Add the sliced onion and sauté until the onion is soft, 3 to 4 minutes. Add the peas, carrots, red bell pepper, tomatoes, and basil. Cook for 1 minute, or until just heated.

Remove from the heat and stir in the rice, turkey, ham, and vinaigrette. Toss to coat completely.

Line a large platter with romaine lettuce leaves and spoon the rice and meat mixture over the lettuce. Sprinkle with green onions and reserved bacon. Serve at once.

BABA GHANOUSH SALAD
(ROASTED EGGPLANT SALAD)

Charring the eggplant on top of the stove and then roasting it in the oven gives it a wonderfully subtle, smoky taste. For an easier recipe, skip the charring step and just roast the eggplant in the oven. Tahini, a paste made of ground sesame seeds, can be found in Middle Eastern markets or large grocery stores.

SERVES 4

2 (1¼ pound) eggplants, unpeeled

2 onions, chopped

4 garlic cloves, chopped

⅓ cup freshly squeezed lemon juice

⅓ cup tahini

2 tablespoons extra-virgin olive oil

1 tablespoon ground cumin

¼ teaspoon cayenne pepper

2 tablespoons chopped parsley

Salt and freshly ground black pepper

2 cups plain low-fat yogurt, drained overnight in a
    strainer lined with cheesecloth

1 cup crumbled feta cheese

¼ cup olive oil

2 tablespoons chopped fresh oregano

1 tablespoon chopped fresh rosemary

1 medium head iceberg lettuce, cored and very thinly sliced

1 pint cherry tomatoes, halved

2 green bell peppers, seeded and cut into strips

½ cup golden raisins

Preheat the oven to 400°F. Place each whole eggplant directly on a gas burner or over a medium flame on the stove top, with the stem pointed away from the flame. Carefully roast for about 5 to 7 minutes, turning with tongs every minute or so, until the skin is blistered and charred.

Remove the eggplants and prick all over with a fork. Wrap each eggplant in foil and seal tightly. Place on the middle rack of the preheated oven and bake for 30 minutes. Unwrap the eggplant carefully (to avoid steam burns). When cool enough to handle, remove and discard the stem and the skin. Coarsely chop on a cutting board, then transfer to a large bowl. Add the onion, garlic, lemon juice, tahini, olive oil, cumin, cayenne pepper, parsley, and salt and pepper to taste.

In a medium bowl stir together the drained yogurt, feta cheese, olive oil, oregano, rosemary, ½ teaspoon of salt, and ½ teaspoon of black pepper.

Divide the lettuce among 4 individual serving plates. Mound the eggplant mixture in the center of the lettuce and surround with cherry tomato halves and green bell pepper strips. Dollop the dressing in the center of the baba ghanoush and garnish with golden raisins. Serve at once.

CLASSIC CAESAR SALAD WITH INTERNATIONAL VARIATIONS

This tasty dressing can be made ahead and refrigerated for up to 7 days. It also makes a delicious dip for fresh crudités or tossed with boiled and sliced new potatoes for a totally different potato salad. I've taken the worry out of using raw eggs in the dressing by substituting a pasteurized egg product. If desired, use 2 egg yolks in place of the egg substitute.

SERVES 4

1 garlic clove

2 to 3 anchovy fillets, drained

1 tablespoon capers, drained

1 teaspoon Dijon mustard

¼ cup thawed egg substitute, very well chilled

¼ cup red wine vinegar

1 teaspoon Worcestershire sauce

⅓ cup vegetable oil

⅓ cup olive oil

1 head romaine lettuce, separated into leaves
     or torn into bite-sized pieces

1 cup freshly grated Parmesan cheese

2 cups Seasoned Croutons (see page 45)

Any of the following optional additions: Grilled shrimp
     or chicken strips, broiled salmon, or sliced roasted lamb,
     beef, or pork

Salt and freshly ground black pepper

In a food processor combine the garlic, anchovies, capers, Dijon mustard, egg substitute, red wine vinegar, and Worcestershire sauce. Process until smooth. With the machine running, add the vegetable oil and olive oil in a thin, steady stream until the mixture is thick and creamy; this process should take about 1 minute.

In a large serving bowl toss the romaine with the dressing, Parmesan cheese, croutons, optional meat or seafood, and salt and pepper to taste. Serve at once.

To the lettuce add 1 cup pitted black olives; 1 seeded and thinly sliced roasted red pepper; 1 cucumber, halved lengthwise, seeded, and cut into crescents; 1 (15$\frac{1}{2}$ ounce) can chickpeas, rinsed and drained; 2 tablespoons chopped fresh oregano; 1 cup crumbled feta cheese; and 1 pound thinly sliced cooked lamb. To the dressing add the juice of 1 lemon. Serve with warm pita bread.

To the lettuce add 2 cups sliced portobello mushrooms, 3 thinly sliced plum tomatoes, 1 (15$\frac{1}{2}$ ounce) can marinated artichoke hearts (drained), 2 tablespoons chopped fresh basil, 1 cup toasted pine nuts, 8 ounces diced fresh mozzarella, and 1 pound grilled shrimp. Serve with warm slices of crostini brushed with olive oil and finely grated Parmesan cheese.

Omit the Parmesan cheese and croutons. To the lettuce add 1 (15$\frac{1}{2}$ ounce) can black beans (rinsed and drained), 1 (8 ounce) can yellow corn (rinsed and drained), 1 (4 ounce) can chopped green chiles, $\frac{1}{2}$ cup chopped fresh cilantro, and 1 pound thinly-sliced, roasted pork tenderloin. To the dressing add 2 tablespoons chopped chipotles in adobo sauce, 1 teaspoon each of chili powder and ground cumin, and the juice of 1 lime. Serve with warm flour tortillas or corn tortilla chips.

Omit the Parmesan cheese and croutons. To the lettuce add 1 (8 ounce) can sliced water chestnuts (rinsed and drained), 2 cups bean sprouts, 1 (8 ounce) can drained straw mushrooms, 1 (16 ounce) can drained pineapple chunks, $\frac{1}{2}$ cup chopped fresh cilantro, $\frac{1}{4}$ cup chopped fresh mint, 1 pound grilled sliced chicken breast or broiled salmon, and 1 cup toasted cashew nuts. To the dressing add 2 tablespoons dark Asian sesame oil, 2 tablespoons soy sauce, and 1 tablespoon chopped fresh ginger. Serve with rice crackers or wafers.

ITALIAN COBB SALAD

This salad is based on the famous Cobb Salad created and served at Hollywood's Brown Derby restaurant during the golden era of film. I've given this a distinctive Italian flair by using ingredients that are indigenous to that country but are easy to find here. With its layers of vibrant colors, the salad makes a stunning presentation.

SERVES 4

1 head romaine lettuce, torn into bite-sized pieces

2 cups pine nuts or walnuts, lightly toasted (see page 9)

8 slices bacon or pancetta, chopped, fried until golden brown, and drained

1 cup diced hard salami

8 ounces Gorgonzola cheese, crumbled (about 2 cups)

2 red bell peppers, seeded and diced

2 green bell peppers, seeded and diced

1 (16 ounce) jar marinated artichoke hearts, drained and diced

4 to 6 Roma tomatoes, seeded and diced (about 2 cups)

2 fennel bulbs, cored and diced

1 red onion, diced

Black olives for garnish

¼ cup oil-packed sun-dried tomatoes, drained and chopped

2 garlic cloves, chopped

⅓ cup balsamic vinegar

⅔ cup extra-virgin olive oil

2 tablespoons chopped fresh basil

½ teaspoon sugar

Salt and freshly ground black pepper

Place the romaine in a large salad bowl. Arrange in successive layers the pine nuts or walnuts, bacon or pancetta and salami, Gorgonzola, red and green bell pepper, diced artichokes, tomatoes, fennel, and red onion on top of the romaine. Place black olives in the center of the salad.

In a small bowl whisk together the sun-dried tomatoes, garlic, balsamic vinegar, olive oil, basil, sugar, and salt and pepper to taste.

Bring the salad and the dressing to the table. Just before serving drizzle the vinaigrette over the salad and toss to coat completely.

Note: The salad can be assembled, tightly wrapped, and refrigerated 4 to 6 hours in advance. Toss with the dressing at the table just before serving.

TANDOORI-STYLE CHICKEN SALAD WITH RAITA CUCUMBER DRESSING

Indian tandoori ovens produce a very dry heat that results in succulent meats, moist and tender on the inside and seared with flavor on the outside. This marinade helps the home cook achieve something similar. Toasting the spices adds another layer of flavor to the finished chicken. You can substitute pork or lamb for the chicken with equally incredible results.

SERVES 4

1 teaspoon ground cumin

1 teaspoon ground coriander

1 teaspoon ground ginger

1 teaspoon ground cardamom

1 teaspoon cayenne pepper

1 teaspoon salt

1 teaspoon black pepper

½ teaspoon ground turmeric

1 small onion, peeled and cut into quarters

2 garlic cloves

1 jalapeño or serrano pepper, seeded and chopped

1 tablespoon chopped fresh ginger

1 cup plain low-fat yogurt

Raita Cucumber Dressing (recipe follows)

4 boneless, skinless chicken breasts

6 cups mesclun

6 cups spinach leaves, stemmed

1 red onion, thinly sliced

1 (15½ ounce) can sliced beets, drained

½ cup golden raisins

½ cup sliced almonds, toasted (see page 9)

In a small skillet over medium heat combine the cumin, coriander, ginger, cardamom, cayenne pepper, salt, pepper, and turmeric. Stir constantly until mixture just begins to smoke. Remove from the heat and set aside.

In a food processor combine the onion, garlic, jalapeño or serrano pepper, and ginger. Pulse until finely chopped. Add the toasted spices and the yogurt. Process until smooth. Place the chicken in a baking dish and top with the yogurt marinade. Cover and refrigerate for at least 1 hour, or overnight.

Preheat the broiler for 15 minutes. Remove the chicken and place on a broiler rack. Broil the chicken, about 6 inches from the heat source, for about 15 minutes, turning once after 7 to 8 minutes. Remove to a cutting board and allow to rest for 10 minutes. Cut the chicken into slices on a diagonal.

In a large bowl toss together the mesclun, spinach, and red onion. Divide among 4 individual serving plates. Place the sliced beets and chicken strips on the greens. Ladle the dressing over the salad and top with golden raisins and almonds.

RAITA CUCUMBER DRESSING

1½ cups plain low-fat yogurt

¼ cup freshly squeezed lemon juice

2 tablespoons chopped fresh cilantro

2 tablespoon chopped fresh mint

2 tablespoons chopped fresh dill

2 shallots, minced

1 cucumber, halved lengthwise, seeded, and cut into ½-inch dice

Salt and freshly ground black pepper to taste

In a medium bowl combine all ingredients. Cover and refrigerate for at least 1 hour, or overnight.

PHILLY CHEESE STEAK SALAD
WITH PEPPERCORN DRESSING

This is one of my favorite Friday night suppers to put together after a hectic week. It's ready in no time and seems to be just the right choice to kick off the much-anticipated weekend.

SERVES 4

¾ cup sour cream

½ cup mayonnaise

2 tablespoons freshly squeezed lemon juice

1 tablespoon prepared horseradish

1 tablespoon Worcestershire sauce

2 tablespoons brine-cured green peppercorns, drained and slightly crushed

3 tablespoons butter

3 tablespoons olive oil

2 garlic cloves, chopped

2 pounds sirloin steak or London broil, very thinly sliced on the diagonal

Salt and freshly ground black pepper

1 large Vidalia onion, thinly sliced

2 green bell peppers, seeded and thinly sliced

¼ cup chopped fresh parsley

4 hoagie-style rolls, split in half lengthwise and lightly toasted

¼ cup balsamic vinegar

2 cups arugula leaves

2 cups thinly sliced radicchio

2 cups curly endive, torn into bite-sized pieces

1½ cups finely grated Gruyère cheese

½ cup freshly grated Parmesan cheese

Make the dressing: In a small bowl whisk together the sour cream, mayonnaise, lemon juice, horseradish, Worcestershire sauce, and green peppercorns. Set aside.

In a 12-inch skillet melt the butter with the olive oil over medium-high heat. When the mixture is hot stir in the garlic and slices of beef. Stir fry for 3 to 4 minutes, or until the slices are medium-rare. Remove with a slotted spoon and place in a large bowl. Season to taste with salt and pepper.

Add the onion and green bell pepper to the skillet and cook until crisp-tender, 2 to 3 minutes. Add the contents of the skillet along with the parsley to the bowl with the sautéed steak and toss to mix. Cover with aluminum foil to keep warm.

Place 1 toasted hoagie half on each of 4 individual serving plates. Brush the rolls with the balsamic vinegar. In a large bowl toss together the arugula, radicchio, and curly endive. Arrange the lettuces on top of the rolls, completely covering the rolls. Spoon the meat and vegetables over the lettuce and top with Gruyère cheese. Spoon some of the dressing over each salad and sprinkle with Parmesan cheese. Top with the remaining hoagie halves, setting them slightly askew. Serve at once.

COD SALAD NIÇOISE

The traditional version of this salad uses canned oil-packed tuna, which is absolutely delicious paired with the other ingredients, but substituting delicate fillets of sautéed cod makes this a really special occasion salad.

SERVES 4

1 tablespoon coarse-grained Dijon mustard

Grated zest of 1 lemon

Juice of 1 lemon

2 tablespoons red wine vinegar

2 shallots, chopped

1/2 cup plus 2 tablespoons extra-virgin olive oil, divided

2 tablespoons chopped fresh basil

1 tablespoon fresh thyme leaves

1 teaspoon sugar

Salt and freshly ground black pepper

1 pound green beans, tipped and tailed

1 pound new potatoes, peeled and thinly sliced

2 tablespoons butter

4 (6 ounce) cod fillets, patted dry

1 large head Boston lettuce, separated into leaves

3/4 cup finely grated Parmesan cheese

2 vine-ripened tomatoes, quartered

4 hard-cooked eggs, peeled and halved lengthwise (see page 33)

1 can oil-packed anchovy fillets, drained

1/2 cup niçoise olives, pitted

2 tablespoons capers, rinsed and drained

3 green onions, chopped

Make the lemon vinaigrette: In a medium bowl mix together the Dijon mustard, lemon zest, lemon juice, red wine vinegar, and shallots. Slowly whisk in 1/2 cup of the olive oil until the dressing is thick and emulsified. Stir in the basil, thyme, sugar, and salt and pepper to taste.

In a 2 1/2-quart saucepan combine the green beans with enough lightly-salted water to cover by 3 inches. Bring to boil, reduce heat to a simmer, and cook for 3 to 4 minutes. Add the potatoes and continue cooking for 3 to 4 minutes, or until the beans are crisp-tender and the potatoes pierce easily with a fork. Drain and toss with 1/4 cup of the lemon vinaigrette.

In a 10-inch skillet set over medium-high heat, heat the butter and remaining 2 tablespoons of olive oil. Lightly season the cod fillets with salt and pepper. Add the cod to the skillet and cook for about 2 minutes per side, or until the fish flakes easily with a fork.

To assemble the salad, line a large platter with Boston lettuce leaves. Drizzle the lettuce with a couple of table-spoons of the lemon vinaigrette. Sprinkle with Parmesan cheese. Mound the green beans and potatoes in the center of the lettuce. Arrange the quartered tomatoes and the cod fillets around the circumference of the serving platter and drizzle with a little of the vinaigrette. Place the eggs around the green beans and potatoes. Place a whole anchovy on top of each egg. Scatter the rest of the anchovies over the salad. Spoon the remaining vinaigrette over the salad. Scatter the olives, capers, and green onions over the salad. Season once again with a little salt and a generous grinding of fresh pepper. Serve at once.

SAUTÉED RATATOUILLE SALAD WITH MINUTE BEEF STEAKS

Minute steaks, sometimes labeled "breakfast steaks," help make this salad easy to prepare. Substituting a 10-ounce package of prewashed mixed spinach greens for the lettuces cuts preparation time even more.

SERVES 4

1 small eggplant, cut into ½-inch dice

Kosher salt

8 minute beef steaks (about 2 to 3 ounces each)

2 tablespoons Worcestershire sauce

½ cup olive oil, divided

1 zucchini, halved lengthwise and sliced in crescents

1 yellow squash, halved lengthwise and sliced in crescents

1 onion, thinly sliced

1 red bell pepper, seeded and sliced

1 green bell pepper, seeded and sliced

4 plum tomatoes, seeded and cut into wedges

4 garlic cloves, chopped

½ cup assorted chopped fresh herbs such as thyme, basil, parsley, oregano, and rosemary, divided

¼ cup balsamic vinegar

1 tablespoon Dijon mustard

1 teaspoon sugar

½ teaspoon salt

½ teaspoon black pepper

6 cups baby spinach leaves

1 cup sliced radicchio

2 cups curly endive, torn into bite-sized pieces

⅔ cup shaved Parmesan cheese

Place the eggplant in a colander and sprinkle with kosher salt. Leave for 30 minutes. Rinse, drain, and pat the eggplant dry.

Preheat the broiler. Line a baking sheet with heavy-duty aluminum foil. Place the beef steaks between 2 sheets of plastic wrap and pound with a meat mallet to a thickness of about ¼ inch. Remove steaks from the plastic wrap and place on the foil-lined baking sheet. Drizzle with Worcestershire sauce. Broil, about 4 inches from the heat source, 1 to 2 minutes, or until cooked through. Remove from the oven and thinly slice into strips.

In a large wok or 12-inch deep skillet, heat ¼ cup of the olive oil over medium-high heat until sizzling. Add the eggplant, zucchini, and squash and sauté for 2 minutes. Add the onion, red and green bell peppers, tomatoes, and garlic. Cook for 3 to 5 minutes, or until crisp-tender. Stir in half of the chopped herbs and remove from the heat.

Make the vinaigrette: In a small bowl or jar with a tight-fitting lid combine the remaining chopped herbs with the remaining ¼ cup of olive oil, balsamic vinegar, Dijon mustard, sugar, salt, and pepper. Whisk or shake until thoroughly combined.

In a large bowl combine the baby spinach, radicchio, and curly endive. Divide the lettuces among 4 individual serving plates. Spoon the sautéed vegetables over the greens, top with the strips of steak and drizzle with the vinaigrette. Scatter the Parmesan shavings over the salad. Serve at once.

SESAME & GINGER VEGETABLE & GARLIC BEEF SALAD

This is an intriguing salad version of a classic stir-fry dish. The zucchini, yellow squash, and carrots can be thinly cut into ribbons using a mandolin or the food processor with a 1 or 2 mm disc. Hoisin sauce is a spicy sweet condiment (primarily made of sweet potatoes, soybeans, soy sauce, honey, and chiles) used in time-honored Asian dishes such as Peking Duck and Moo Shu Pork.

SERVES 4

3 tablespoons butter

3 tablespoons olive oil

2 garlic cloves, chopped

¼ cup chopped parsley

2 pounds sirloin steak, very thinly sliced on the diagonal

Salt and freshly ground black pepper

1 large Vidalia onion, thinly sliced

1 red bell pepper, seeded and thinly sliced

1 green bell pepper, seeded and thinly sliced

2 zucchini, thinly sliced lengthwise

2 yellow squash, thinly sliced lengthwise

3 carrots, shaved into ribbons using a vegetable peeler

3 tablespoons chopped fresh ginger

3 tablespoons sesame seeds

⅓ cup dry sherry or chicken stock

2 tablespoons dark Asian sesame oil

⅔ cup hoisin sauce

⅓ cup soy sauce

¼ cup freshly squeezed orange juice

2 tablespoons honey

1 tablespoon Chinese or Dijon mustard

2 green onions, chopped

1 to 2 teaspoons Chinese chile garlic paste

⅓ cup chopped fresh cilantro

In a large wok or 12-inch skillet melt the butter with the olive oil over medium-high heat. When the mixture is hot stir in the garlic and parsley. Stir fry for 30 seconds. Add the beef strips and continue to cook for 3 to 4 minutes, or until the strips are medium-rare. Season to taste with salt and pepper.

In a microwave-safe bowl toss the onion, red and green bell peppers, zucchini, yellow squash, carrots, ginger, sesame seeds, dry sherry or chicken stock, and sesame oil. Season to taste with salt and pepper. Cover tightly with plastic wrap. With a knife, make 3 to 4 slits in the plastic wrap to allow steam to escape. Place in the microwave and cook on high power for 3 to 4 minutes, or until crisp tender. (Check your microwave manual for specific cooking requirements for your appliance.) Carefully remove the wrap away from your face to avoid any steam burns. (Alternately, toss these ingredients together in a large bowl and transfer them to a steamer basket. Steam the vegetables for 4 to 5 minutes, or until they are crisp-tender.)

Make the hoisin dressing: In a small bowl whisk together the hoisin sauce, soy sauce, orange juice, honey, mustard, green onions, and chile garlic paste.

With a slotted spoon divide the vegetables among 4 individual serving plates. Decoratively arrange the beef strips over the vegetables. Spoon the hoisin dressing over the salad and top with chopped cilantro. Serve at once.

ASIAN CABBAGE SALAD WITH STIR-FRIED PORK & PEANUTS

Is it salad or a stir-fry? What's the difference? It's delicious! By the way, this is one of my most requested recipes among my students, even if I can't put it in a particular category. I guess some things in life are not to be questioned!

SERVES 4

2 cups thinly sliced bok choy

1 large Vidalia onion, thinly sliced

2 carrots, shredded

1 (16 ounce) can pineapple chunks in juice, drained (reserve juice)

½ English cucumber, halved, seeded, and thinly sliced into crescents

¼ cup sugar

1 tablespoon dry mustard

½ cup apple cider vinegar

3 tablespoons peanut butter

2 tablespoons soy sauce

¼ cup ketchup

¼ cup reserved pineapple juice

2 tablespoons dark Asian sesame oil

⅓ cup chopped fresh cilantro

1 tablespoon sesame seeds, lightly toasted (see page 9)

1 teaspoon celery seeds

Salt and freshly ground black pepper

2 tablespoons peanut oil

2 garlic cloves, chopped

1 tablespoon chopped fresh ginger

1 pound pork tenderloin, very thinly sliced

½ small head Napa cabbage, cored and very thinly sliced

½ small head red cabbage, cored and very thinly sliced

½ cup chopped peanuts, lightly toasted (see page 9)

In a large bowl combine the bok choy, Vidalia onion, carrots, pineapple chunks, and cucumber.

Make the dressing: In a food processor combine the sugar, dry mustard, apple cider vinegar, peanut butter, soy sauce, ketchup, pineapple juice, and sesame oil. Process until smooth. Add the cilantro, sesame seeds, celery seeds, and salt and pepper to taste. Pulse just until mixture is blended thoroughly.

Heat a wok over medium-high heat for 5 minutes. Add the peanut oil and swirl to coat the wok. Add the garlic and ginger and cook for 30 seconds. Add the pork tenderloin slices and continue cooking for 2 to 3 minutes, or until the pork is no longer pink. Add the vegetables and the dressing. Cook until the bok choy and Vidalia onion begin to wilt ever so slightly, about 2 minutes. Do not overcook.

Arrange the Napa and red cabbage on a large serving platter. Spoon the contents of the wok over the cabbage. Garnish with chopped peanuts. Serve warm or at room temperature.

JACK CHEESE QUESADILLA SALAD WITH CILANTRO LIME VINAIGRETTE

For variety, add smoked chicken, crab meat, or chopped steamed shrimp to the filling mixture.

SERVES 4

¼ cup sour cream

1 (3 ounce) package cream cheese, softened

4 green onions, chopped

½ cup plus 2 tablespoons chopped fresh cilantro

1 teaspoon chili powder

½ teaspoon ground cumin

1 jalapeño pepper, seeded and finely chopped

½ cup grated sharp cheddar cheese

1 cup grated Monterey Jack cheese

Salt and freshly ground black pepper

8 (10 inch) flour tortillas

1 egg white, beaten until frothy

Peanut or vegetable oil for brushing the skillet

Juice of 3 limes

2 garlic cloves, chopped

1 teaspoon honey

¼ teaspoon red pepper flakes

½ cup peanut oil

8 cups mesclun

1 jicama, peeled and cut into 2-inch matchsticks

1 red onion, thinly sliced

1 ruby red grapefruit, peeled and cut into sections,
   seeds removed

1 (4 ounce) can sliced black olives, drained

In a large bowl combine the sour cream, cream cheese, green onions, 2 tablespoons of the chopped cilantro, chili powder, cumin, jalapeño pepper, cheddar cheese, Monterey Jack cheese, and salt and pepper to taste.

Place ½ cup of the mixture on a tortilla and spread to within ½ inch of the edge. Brush the edge of the tortilla with the beaten egg white and place a second tortilla on top, pressing to seal the edges. Repeat with the remaining tortillas.

Lightly brush peanut or vegetable oil onto the bottom of a 12-inch nonstick skillet. Heat the skillet over medium-high heat until sizzling hot. Reduce the heat to medium and quickly cook the tortillas, turning once, 1 to 2 minutes per side. Remove from the pan, place on paper towels, and tent with aluminum foil to keep warm.

Make the cilantro lime vinaigrette: In a small bowl whisk together the lime juice, garlic, the remaining ¼ cup of chopped cilantro, honey, red pepper flakes, and ½ cup of peanut oil. Taste, adding salt and pepper as needed.

Divide the mesclun, jicama, red onion, and grapefruit among 4 individual salad plates. Cut each quesadilla into 8 wedges and arrange around the salad. Drizzle the vinaigrette over the greens, top with the sliced black olives, and serve at once.

WARM GERMAN POTATO SALAD WITH SAUSAGES & CARAWAY VINAIGRETTE

I like this delicious salad supper best in the fall, after a day spent outdoors with my dogs, Gypsy and Cagney.

SERVES 4

1 tablespoon coarse-grained Dijon mustard

¼ cup apple cider vinegar

1 shallot, chopped

2 tablespoons prepared horseradish

½ cup olive oil

1 tablespoon caraway seeds, crushed

2 teaspoons dried marjoram leaves

1 teaspoon ground ginger

½ teaspoon ground allspice

Dash of freshly grated nutmeg

2 tablespoons brown sugar

½ teaspoon salt

½ teaspoon black pepper

2 pounds medium-sized red new potatoes, scrubbed
   and thickly sliced

2 ribs of celery, thinly sliced

1 cup thinly sliced radishes

1 (15½ ounce) can white beans, rinsed and drained

1 (8 ounce) can sauerkraut, rinsed and drained

8 strips of bacon, coarsely chopped

2 yellow onions, chopped

1 cup apple juice

3 tablespoons vegetable oil

6 large fresh bratwurst sausages, pricked all over with a fork

1 red onion, thinly sliced

1 red bell pepper, seeded and thinly sliced

1 (12 ounce) bottle of dark beer or 1½ cups apple juice

1 cup shredded Gruyère cheese

¼ cup chopped parsley

Preheat the oven to 200°F.

Make the caraway vinaigrette: In a medium bowl whisk together the Dijon mustard, apple cider vinegar, shallot, horseradish, olive oil, caraway seeds, marjoram, ginger, allspice, nutmeg, brown sugar, salt, and pepper.

In a 3½-quart Dutch oven cover the potatoes with enough lightly salted water to cover them by 3 inches. Bring the water to the boil and cook the potatoes for 10 minutes, or until just tender. Drain and place in an oven-proof bowl. Add the celery, radishes, white beans, and sauerkraut. Toss gently. Cover the bowl with aluminum foil to keep the potatoes warm.

In a 12-inch skillet set over medium-high heat fry the bacon until crisp and browned. Drain on paper towels and set aside. Return the skillet to the heat, reduce the heat to medium, add the yellow onion to the hot drippings, and cook for 5 minutes, or until soft. Add the vinaigrette, and 1 cup of apple juice and cook until the mixture has reduced by half, 7 to 8 minutes. Immediately pour the hot dressing over the potato salad and gently toss, being careful not to break the potatoes. Cover once again with aluminum foil and place in the oven to keep warm.

In the same skillet heat the vegetable oil over medium-high heat. Add the sausages to the hot skillet and cook, using tongs to turn them until well browned all over, about 10 minutes. Add the red onion, red bell pepper, and beer or apple juice to the skillet. Bring to a boil and cook, partially covered, for 12 to 15 minutes, or until the sausages are cooked through completely and the liquid has evaporated.

Remove the warm potato salad from the oven and transfer to a serving platter. Top with the sausages and sautéed vegetables. Sprinkle with Gruyère cheese and parsley. Garnish with the crispy bacon.

QUICK SALADS
(30 MINUTES OR LESS)

Spicy Thai Chicken Salad with Lime Coconut Dressing

Classic Basil, Tomato, and Mozzarella Platter with Prosciutto

Tuscan Cherry Tomato and Bread Salad (Panzanella)

Penne Pasta Vegetable Salad with Peanut Dressing

Middle Eastern Couscous and Green Olive Salad

Garlicky Greek Salad with Anchovy and Feta Vinaigrette

Quick Quinoa Salad

Asian Noodle Salad

Mesclun with Smoked Salmon, Caper Cream Cheese Dressing, and Bagel Croutons

Colorful Salmon and Couscous Salad

Country Ham, Bitter Greens, and Apple Salad with Honey Bacon Vinaigrette

SPICY THAI CHICKEN SALAD WITH LIME COCONUT DRESSING

I adapted this salad from one created by my good friend, Virginia Willis, who is now the kitchen director for Martha Stewart. Virginia demonstrated this recipe in a Thai class she taught at my cooking school in Atlanta. It combines and balances the four flavor components of Thai cuisine: sweet, salty, sour, and spicy.

SERVES 4

2 small dried red chiles, broken into pieces

¼ cup hot water

2 tablespoons brown sugar

½ teaspoon ground cumin

½ teaspoon ground coriander

1 small yellow onion, finely chopped

½ teaspoon black pepper

2 tablespoons cilantro leaves

2 tablespoons chopped fresh basil

A 2-inch piece of lemongrass

2 tablespoons chopped fresh ginger

4 garlic cloves, peeled

1 tablespoon shrimp paste (optional)

2 tablespoons freshly squeezed lime juice

⅔ cup unsweetened coconut milk

4 kaffir lime leaves

1 teaspoon paprika

1 tablespoon fish sauce

4 boneless, skinless chicken breasts, cut into very thin strips

1 red bell pepper, seeded and cut into ⅛-inch strips

8 cups mesclun

½ cup chopped peanuts

4 green onions, chopped

2 tablespoons chopped fresh mint

1 lime, cut into 4 wedges

In a food processor purée the dried chiles, water, brown sugar, cumin, coriander, onion, black pepper, cilantro, basil, lemongrass, ginger, garlic, optional shrimp paste, and lime juice.

In a 10-inch, deep skillet over medium heat, heat the coconut milk to a gentle simmer. Add the kaffir lime leaves, paprika, fish sauce, and the puréed mixture. Stir well to combine. Add the chicken strips and cook for 8 to 10 minutes, or until the chicken is just cooked. Add the red bell pepper and cook 1 to 2 minutes longer, or until pepper is crisp-tender.

While the chicken strips are cooking, place the mesclun on individual serving plates or a large platter. With a slotted spoon remove the chicken and red bell pepper from the sauce. Arrange them on top of the greens. Bring the sauce remaining in the skillet to a boil and cook until it is reduced by about one-third. Remove and discard the lime leaves. Drizzle the salad with the reduced sauce. Top with chopped peanuts, green onions, and mint. Serve immediately, with wedges of lime.

Note: Lemongrass, shrimp paste, coconut milk, fish sauce, and kaffir lime leaves can now be found in the specialty or international food section of many large grocery stores, farmers markets, and Asian food shops.

CLASSIC BASIL, TOMATO, & MOZZARELLA PLATTER WITH PROSCIUTTO

Freshness is the key to this simple luncheon salad. Choose firm vine-ripened tomatoes, the kind dripping with juice, not the mealy, pale pink supermarket variety.

SERVES 4

4 large, very ripe tomatoes, cut into ¼-inch-thick slices

1 pound fresh mozzarella cheese, cut into 24 thin slices

1 pound thinly sliced proscuitto ham, each slice folded accordion-style, like a pleated fan

24 large basil leaves, washed and patted dry

3 green onions, chopped

1 tablespoon capers, rinsed and drained

1 tablespoon chopped fresh oregano

3 tablespoons extra-virgin olive oil

3 tablespoons balsamic vinegar

Salt and freshly ground black pepper

½ cup shaved Parmesan cheese

Additional basil leaves for garnish

On a large round platter, alternately layer the tomato slices, mozzarella slices, proscuitto slices, and whole basil leaves, overlapping in a circular pattern.

Sprinkle with the green onions, capers, oregano, olive oil, balsamic vinegar, and salt and pepper to taste. Garnish with the shaved Parmesan cheese and additional basil leaves and serve at room temperature.

TUSCAN CHERRY TOMATO & BREAD SALAD
(PANZANELLA)

This easy salad comes together in minutes. Be sure to use a firm-textured bread or the salad will become mushy and lose its characteristic chewy and crunchy textures. Sweet cherry tomatoes, available throughout the year, make this a treat in any season.

SERVES 4

10 (1½-inch-thick) slices stale firm-textured Italian bread

4 cups vegetable stock or water

1 red onion, sliced

1 English cucumber, diced

1 green bell pepper, seeded and thinly sliced

1 pint cherry tomatoes, halved

1 cup tightly-packed basil leaves

1 cup pitted brine-cured black olives

12 oil-packed anchovy fillets, coarsely chopped

¼ cup capers, rinsed and drained

Salt and freshly ground black pepper

½ cup extra-virgin olive oil

¼ cup red wine vinegar

1 cup shaved Romano cheese

In a large bowl soak the bread in the vegetable stock or water for 5 minutes. Squeeze out the excess stock or water and discard any leftover liquid. Tear the soaked bread into bite-sized pieces.

In a large bowl toss together the bread, red onion, cucumber, green bell pepper, cherry tomatoes, basil leaves, black olives, anchovies, capers, and salt and pepper to taste. Drizzle with the olive oil and red wine vinegar. Toss gently. Top with the Romano cheese and serve at once.

PENNE PASTA VEGETABLE SALAD
WITH PEANUT DRESSING

Any short pasta works well in this recipe so have fun experimenting with rigatoni, farfalle, shell pasta, or elbow macaroni. The delightful dressing is very versatile. Use it also as a dipping sauce for chicken satay, steamed dumplings, or crudités.

SERVES 4

1 small bunch broccoli

½ pound snow peas, tipped and tailed

1 garlic clove, peeled

1 tablespoon chopped fresh ginger

¼ cup chunky peanut butter

¼ cup rice wine vinegar

2 tablespoons soy sauce

1 tablespoon dark Asian sesame oil

½ teaspoon red pepper flakes

1 teaspoon sugar

¼ cup chopped fresh cilantro

Juice of 1 lime

12 ounces penne pasta, cooked according to package directions
   and drained

1 red bell pepper, seeded and thinly sliced

1 yellow bell pepper, seeded and thinly sliced

3 carrots, shredded

3 green onions, chopped

½ cup chopped roasted peanuts

1 small cucumber, seeded and diced

Cut the broccoli into florets. Blanch the broccoli and snow peas in lightly salted, boiling water for 30 seconds, drain, and refresh under cold water running water to stop the cooking. Set aside.

Make the peanut dressing: In a food processor combine the garlic, ginger, peanut butter, rice wine vinegar, soy sauce, dark Asian sesame oil, red pepper flakes, and sugar. Process until smooth. Add the chopped cilantro and lime juice and pulse just to combine.

In a large bowl combine the blanched broccoli and snow peas, cooked penne, red bell pepper, yellow bell pepper, carrots, and green onions. Toss with the peanut sauce and chill for at least 2 hours.

When ready to serve, toss once again and sprinkle with the chopped peanuts and diced cucumber. Serve chilled or at room temperature.

MIDDLE EASTERN COUSCOUS & GREEN OLIVE SALAD

*Couscous is actually a pasta made from semolina flour. It is a pantry staple in my house
and fills out my impromptu summertime menus in a flash.*

SERVES 4

3½ cups chicken stock

1 tablespoon ground cumin

6 green onions, chopped

1 red bell pepper, seeded and chopped

1 cup sliced button mushrooms

Grated zest of 1 lemon

⅓ cup plus 2 tablespoons freshly squeezed lemon juice, divided

1½ cups couscous

1 cup thinly sliced green olives with pimentos

6 anchovy fillets, chopped

2 garlic cloves, finely chopped

2 tablespoons capers, rinsed and drained

¼ cup chopped fresh basil

1 cup chopped pistachio nuts, lightly toasted (see page 9)

Salt and freshly ground black pepper

1 head romaine lettuce, separated into whole leaves

⅓ cup extra-virgin olive oil

2 tablespoons chopped parsley

1 cup crumbled feta cheese

In a 2½-quart saucepan heat the chicken stock to boiling. Stir in the cumin, green onions, red bell pepper, mushrooms, lemon zest, and 2 tablespoons of the lemon juice. Cook for 3 minutes. Remove from the heat, add the couscous, stir, and cover. Let sit for 5 minutes. Remove the cover and fluff the couscous with a fork.

Stir in the green olives, anchovies, garlic, capers, basil, pistachio nuts, and salt and pepper to taste.

Line a large platter with romaine leaves. Mound the couscous on the lettuce and drizzle with the remaining ⅓ cup of lemon juice and the olive oil. Sprinkle with the parsley and feta cheese just before serving.

GARLICKY GREEK SALAD WITH ANCHOVY & FETA VINAIGRETTE

The feta and oregano in the vinaigrette give this salad a distinctive Greek flavor, while the oranges add a delicate sweetness. For more robust appetites, top the salad with skewered lamb kebabs.

SERVES 4

1 large eggplant, cut into ³⁄₄-inch cubes

1 large zucchini, halved lengthwise and cut into ¹⁄₂-inch crescents

2 tablespoons olive oil

2 tablespoons chopped fresh mint

Salt and freshly ground black pepper

¹⁄₂ (10 ounce) package prewashed spinach, stems removed (about 6 cups)

1 red onion, thinly sliced and separated into rings

2 navel oranges, peeled and thinly sliced

1 red bell pepper, seeded and thinly sliced

1 cup pitted Greek black olives

¹⁄₄ cup white wine vinegar

1 tablespoon Dijon mustard

2 tablespoons chopped fresh oregano

4 garlic cloves, chopped

¹⁄₄ cup capers, rinsed and drained

1 teaspoon sugar

²⁄₃ cup extra-virgin olive oil

1 cup crumbled feta cheese

8 anchovy fillets, chopped

¹⁄₂ cup whole peperoncini peppers

Preheat the oven to 400°F. In a large bowl toss together the eggplant, zucchini, olive oil, mint, and salt and pepper to taste. Spread the mixture on a foil-lined baking sheet. Roast in the oven for 20 minutes, or until soft. Remove from the oven and allow to cool.

On a large serving platter arrange the spinach, red onions, oranges slices, cooked vegetables, red bell pepper, and black olives.

In a small bowl combine the white wine vinegar, Dijon mustard, oregano, garlic, capers, ¹⁄₂ teaspoon of salt, ¹⁄₂ teaspoon of black pepper, and sugar. Slowly whisk in the olive oil in a thin, steady stream. Stir in the feta cheese and anchovies. Drizzle the vinaigrette over the salad, garnish with the peperoncini peppers, and serve at once.

QUICK QUINOA SALAD

Quinoa was a staple grain of the Inca tribes of ancient Peru. Today it can be found in most large grocery stores or farmer's markets. Long-grained rice, couscous, wild rice, or brown rice can be substituted for the quinoa. Simply adjust the liquid and cooking time according to the package directions.

SERVES 4

3 cups vegetable stock

1½ cups quinoa, rinsed very well

1 (10 ounce) package English peas, thawed

2 tablespoons butter

2 carrots, shredded

2 zucchini, halved lengthwise and thinly sliced

1 red onion, chopped

1 (15½ ounce) can red kidney beans, rinsed and drained

4 plum tomatoes, seeded and diced

3 tablespoons chopped fresh dill

¼ cup red wine vinegar

1 teaspoon Dijon mustard

1 garlic clove, chopped

⅔ cup olive oil

½ teaspoon salt

½ teaspoon black pepper

½ teaspoon sugar

1 cup crumbled feta cheese

⅔ cup chopped pecans, lightly toasted (see page 9)

In a 2½-quart saucepan bring the vegetable stock to a boil. Reduce the heat to medium and stir in the quinoa. Cover and simmer for 10 to 15 minutes, or until the liquid has been absorbed. Remove from the heat and stir in the peas. Cover and let sit for 5 minutes.

In a 10-inch skillet set over medium-high heat, melt the butter. Add the carrots, zucchini, and red onion. Cook for 5 to 7 minutes, or until the onion is tender.

In a large bowl toss together the contents of the skillet with the quinoa and peas, kidney beans, plum tomatoes, and dill.

In a small bowl whisk together the red wine vinegar, Dijon mustard, garlic, olive oil, salt, pepper, and sugar. Pour the vinaigrette over the salad. Toss to coat.

Divide the salad among 4 individual plates and garnish with feta cheese and pecans.

ASIAN NOODLE SALAD

If you like, double the amount of vinaigrette and use the extra to baste grilled chicken, pork, or salmon.
Cube or shred the meat and add to the salad just before tossing.

SERVES 4

¼ cup rice wine vinegar

¼ cup soy sauce

2 tablespoons dark Asian sesame oil

¼ cup peanut oil

¼ cup Chinese chili oil

1 teaspoon honey

2 tablespoons chopped fresh ginger

¼ cup sesame seeds

1 (16 ounce) package Asian noodles, ramen noodles, or
   spaghetti, cooked according to package directions, drained

1 (10 ounce) package French-cut green beans, blanched for 30
   seconds in boiling water and drained

1 cup fresh bean sprouts

1 (8 ounce) can sliced water chestnuts, rinsed and drained

8 green onions, sliced on the diagonal into 1-inch pieces

1 cucumber, halved lengthwise, seeded, and cut into thin crescents

½ cup chopped fresh cilantro

½ cup chopped roasted peanuts

In a medium bowl or small jar with a tight-fitting lid combine the rice wine vinegar, soy sauce, sesame oil, peanut oil, chili oil, honey, ginger, and sesame seeds. Whisk or shake until well blended.

In a large bowl toss together the noodles, green beans, bean sprouts, water chestnuts, green onions, cucumber, and cilantro. Add the dressing and toss thoroughly. Garnish with chopped peanuts and serve at room temperature.

MESCLUN WITH SMOKED SALMON, CAPER CREAM CHEESE DRESSING, & BAGEL CROUTONS

If you enjoy bagels with lox and cream cheese, this salad is for you. The dressing and the bagel croutons can be made up to a week ahead.

SERVES 4

2 plain or onion bagels, cut in half, each half cut into 12 pieces

Nonstick cooking spray

1 teaspoon dried Italian seasoning

½ teaspoon onion powder

½ teaspoon garlic powder

¼ teaspoon cayenne pepper

1 cup cottage cheese, drained in a sieve lined with cheesecloth for 1 hour

1 (3 ounce) package cream cheese

3 tablespoons pepper-flavored vodka (see note)

2 tablespoons freshly squeezed lemon juice

1 teaspoon Dijon mustard

1 tablespoon prepared horseradish

3 tablespoons chopped fresh dill

2 tablespoons capers, rinsed and drained

Salt and freshly ground black pepper

10 cups mesclun

10 ounces thinly sliced smoked salmon or lox

1 red onion, thinly sliced

1 cucumber, peeled, halved lengthwise, seeded, and cut into thin crescents

4 hard-cooked eggs, peeled and sliced (see page 33)

Preheat the oven to 350°F. Scatter the bagel pieces on a large baking sheet. Spray lightly with nonstick cooking spray. Sprinkle the bagels with dried Italian seasoning, onion powder, garlic powder, and cayenne pepper. Toss to coat completely. Bake for 10 to 12 minutes, or until golden and crisp.

Make the caper cream cheese dressing: In a food processor combine the drained cottage cheese, cream cheese, vodka, lemon juice, mustard, horseradish, and dill. Process until smooth. Transfer the mixture to a small bowl and stir in the capers. Season to taste with salt and pepper.

Divide the mesclun among 4 individual serving plates. Decoratively arrange the smoked salmon, red onion, cucumber, and sliced eggs on top of the lettuce. Drizzle with the dressing and garnish each salad with a handful of bagel croutons. Serve at once.

Notes:

• It's easy to make your own pepper-flavored vodka. In a clean glass bottle mix together 2 cups of vodka, 6 dried hot peppers, 1 tablespoon whole black peppercorns, and 1 teaspoon red pepper flakes. Steep for about 1 week in a cool, dark place, then strain and pour into a clean bottle with a tight-fitting lid. This flavored vodka will last indefinitely.

• You can store the croutons in an airtight container for 1 week, or freeze for 1 month.

COLORFUL SALMON & COUSCOUS SALAD

I created this salad in a hurry one summer night when a stalled tropical storm forced some traveling friends to stay overnight with me. That serendipitous meal turned out to be a pleasant beginning to my friends' vacation itinerary.

SERVES 4

3½ cups chicken stock

1 red onion, thinly sliced

1 green bell pepper, seeded and thinly sliced

1 cup sliced button mushrooms

1 (10 ounce) package frozen English peas, thawed

Juice and grated zest of 1 orange

1½ cups couscous

3 (6 ounce) cans flaked salmon, drained

1 tablespoon Dijon mustard

2 garlic cloves, chopped

¼ cup white balsamic or champagne vinegar

½ cup olive oil

¼ cup chopped fresh basil

Salt and freshly ground black pepper

1 head romaine lettuce, torn into bite-sized pieces

1 tablespoon freshly squeezed lemon juice

1 orange

⅔ cup lightly salted, roasted pistachio nuts (see page 9)

½ cup dried cranberries

In a 2½-quart saucepan bring the chicken stock to a boil. Stir in the red onion, green bell pepper, mushrooms, peas, orange juice, and orange zest. Cook for 3 minutes. Remove from the heat, add the couscous, stir, and cover. Let sit for 5 minutes. Remove the cover and fluff the couscous with a fork. Stir in the flaked salmon.

In a small bowl whisk together the Dijon mustard, garlic, white balsamic or champagne vinegar, olive oil, basil, and salt and pepper to taste. Pour over the couscous and toss to coat.

Line a large platter with romaine lettuce leaves. Drizzle the lettuce with lemon juice. Mound the couscous on the lettuce. With a vegetable peeler or paring knife, peel the skin of the orange, being careful not to peel any of the bitter white or pith. Thinly slice the orange peel into julienne strips. Garnish the salad with the orange peel, pistachio nuts, and dried cranberries. Serve at once.

COUNTRY HAM, BITTER GREENS, & APPLE SALAD WITH HONEY BACON VINAIGRETTE

It is essential for the dressing to remain hot to allow the greens to wilt ever so slightly and develop their full flavor. The apple liqueur drizzled over the salad just before serving intensifies the fruity taste.

SERVES 4

4 slices (about 3 ounces each) country ham

⅓ cup very strong coffee

8 slices of bacon, chopped

2 tablespoons coarse-grained Dijon mustard

1 teaspoon salt

1 teaspoon black pepper

⅓ cup honey

⅓ cup apple cider vinegar

¼ cup apple cider or juice

½ cup extra-virgin olive oil

6 cups torn bitter greens, such as curly endive, arugula, radicchio, and watercress

4 cups baby spinach

1 red onion, thinly sliced

2 Granny Smith or Rome apples, halved, cored, and thinly sliced

1 cup coarsely chopped walnuts, toasted (see page 9)

1 cup shaved Parmesan cheese

2 tablespoons Calvados or Applejack Brandy (optional)

In a 12-inch skillet over medium-high heat, fry the country ham slices until heated through, 2 to 3 minutes per side. Add the coffee and simmer until the liquid has completely evaporated. Remove the country ham and set aside.

In the same skillet over medium-high heat, fry the bacon until golden brown. Remove with a slotted spoon and drain on paper towels.

Make the honey bacon vinaigrette: To the hot drippings add the mustard, salt, pepper, honey, and apple cider vinegar. Bring to a boil and simmer for 1 minute. Add the apple cider or juice and olive oil, whisking until well combined. Reduce the heat to a simmer and keep warm.

In a large salad bowl combine the bitter greens, spinach leaves, onion, and apple slices. Drizzle the dressing over the salad and toss to evenly coat. Let sit for 2 minutes.

Place a ham steak on each of 4 individual serving plates. Top with the wilted salad and sprinkle with walnuts, Parmesan cheese, and crumbled bacon. Drizzle with the Calvados or brandy, if desired, and serve at once.

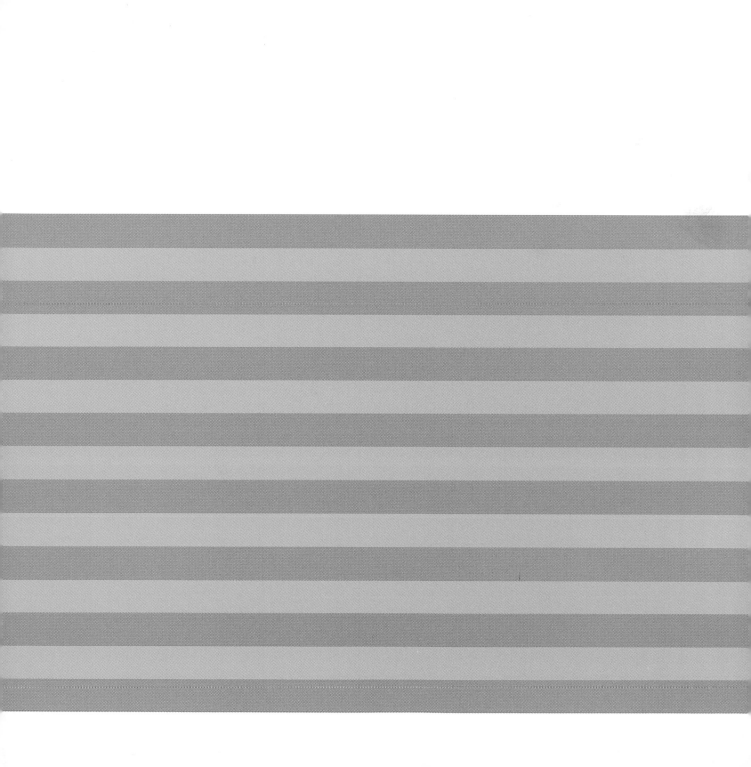

SPECIAL OCCASION SALADS

Warm Chicken Livers with Confetti Vinaigrette

Duck Breast Salad with Sweet and Tart Currant Vinaigrette

Mediterranean Ratatouille Torte on Baby Spinach

Roasted Portobello, Brie, and Arugula Salad with Lemon Pepper Vinaigrette

Spaghetti Squash Salad with Orange Tapenade Vinaigrette

Crab Cakes on Mesclun with Jalapeño Remoulade Dressing

Winter White Salad with Pan-Seared Scallops

Chili-Rubbed Salmon Salad with Cilantro Curry Vinaigrette

Cajun Andouille and Rice Salad with Pecans and Fig Dressing

Roasted Sirloin, Potato, and Mushroom Salad with Roquefort Dressing

Skewered Lamb Salad with Herb Gremolata Dressing

Sausage-Stuffed Onions with Apple Cider Dressing

WARM CHICKEN LIVERS WITH CONFETTI VINAIGRETTE

The confetti vinaigrette is also a marvelous dressing for steamed vegetables or a nice baste for fish, pork, or poultry. It can be made ahead and stored in an airtight container in the refrigerator. Shake or whisk well before using.

2 cups vegetable shortening

1 egg, beaten

½ cup milk

½ teaspoon Tabasco sauce

½ cup yellow cornmeal (not cornmeal mix)

1 cup all-purpose flour

½ teaspoon salt

½ teaspoon black pepper

1 teaspoon poultry seasoning

1 teaspoon paprika

1 teaspoon garlic powder

1 teaspoon onion powder

2 pounds chicken livers (about 36), tough membranes removed, rinsed, and patted dry

1 tablespoon chopped fresh rosemary

1 tablespoon chopped parsley

8 cups mixed baby greens

2 Granny Smith apples, halved, cored, and cut into chunks

1 cup sliced radishes

12 large radicchio leaves

4 green onions, chopped

1 lemon, cut into 4 wedges

Confetti Vinaigrette

1 tablespoon Dijon mustard

2 garlic cloves, chopped

¼ cup chopped red bell pepper

¼ cup chopped green bell pepper

¼ cup chopped yellow bell pepper

1 jalapeño pepper, seeded and chopped

½ cup sherry vinegar

1 cup extra-virgin olive oil

1 teaspoon salt

2 teaspoons sugar

½ tablespoon black pepper

In a 12-inch deep skillet or frying pan, heat the shortening to 360°F. (If you do not have a deep-fat frying thermometer, follow the directions for heating oil on page 49.)

While the shortening is melting, in a small bowl combine the egg, milk, and Tabasco. In a shallow pie plate or dish combine the cornmeal, flour, salt, pepper, poultry seasoning, paprika, garlic powder, and onion powder. Dip the chicken livers into the egg/milk mixture, then dredge in the cornmeal/flour mixture. Place the chicken livers, in batches if necessary, in the frying pan. Allow the pieces to slightly touch, but do not overcrowd the pan. Reduce the heat to medium-high and cook the chicken livers, turning as needed, for 8 to 10 minutes, or until they are a dark, golden brown. Remove and drain on paper towels.

Make the vinaigrette: In a large bowl mix together the mustard, garlic, red bell pepper, green bell pepper, yellow bell pepper, jalapeño pepper, and sherry vinegar. Slowly whisk in the oil. Add the salt, sugar, and pepper. Taste for seasoning and add more according to your taste.

Put the chicken livers in a large bowl and toss them with half of the vinaigrette. Sprinkle with chopped rosemary and parsley. Toss to coat evenly. Let marinate at room temperature for at least 1 hour, or cover and place in the refrigerator for up to 24 hours.

When ready to serve, toss together the mixed baby greens, apple chunks, and radishes with the remaining vinaigrette. Divide the lettuce mixture among 4 individual serving plates. Nestle 3 radicchio leaves in the center of each plate to form a cup. Place the marinated livers in the radicchio leaves. Garnish with green onions, and squeeze lemon wedge over each salad just before serving.

DUCK BREAST SALAD WITH SWEET
& TART CURRANT VINAIGRETTE

As an alternative to broiling, the duck breasts can be grilled, skin sides down, over hot coals, or pan-fried in 3 tablespoons of butter over medium heat for the same amount of time. Do not overcook the breasts, as they will become very dry and tough.

SERVES 4

4 boned duck breasts with skin, about 6 ounces each

Salt and freshly ground black pepper

¼ cup apple cider vinegar

1 tablespoon Dijon mustard

3 tablespoons red currant jelly

1 tablespoon chopped fresh rosemary

½ cup extra-virgin olive oil

⅓ cup dried currants or raisins

6 cups mesclun

6 cups spinach leaves, stemmed

1½ cups fresh blueberries, divided

1½ cups cashews or hazelnuts, lightly toasted
   (see page 9), divided

4 green onions, chopped

Preheat the broiler. Season the duck breasts with salt and pepper. Place the duck on a broiler rack and broil, about 6 inches from the heat source, turning once, until medium rare, about 4 minutes per side. Remove from the oven to a cutting board and tent with aluminum foil to stay warm.

Make the vinaigrette: In a food processor process the apple cider vinegar, Dijon mustard, red currant jelly, ½ teaspoon of salt, ½ teaspoon of black pepper, and rosemary until smooth. With the machine running, add the olive oil in a thin, steady stream until the vinaigrette is thick and emulsified. Add the the dried currants or raisins and pulse just to combine.

Toss the mesclun, spinach, 1 cup of the blueberries, and 1 cup of the cashews or hazelnuts with enough vinaigrette to lightly coat the greens. Arrange the salad on 4 individual serving plates. Cut each duck breast crosswise on a diagonal into thin strips and arrange on top of the dressed greens. Ladle the remaining vinaigrette over the duck. Garnish with the remaining blueberries, cashews or hazelnuts, and green onions.

MEDITERRANEAN RATATOUILLE
TORTE ON BABY SPINACH

A quick trip to the local farm stand inspired this special occasion salad, which I first made last summer at my friend Nancy's house on Long Island. Buy the best balsamic vinegar, olive oil, goat cheese, and Parmesan cheese your budget allows.

SERVES 4

1 (16 ounce) bottle good-quality balsamic vinegar

1 tablespoon honey

1 large eggplant, sliced lengthwise into 8 slices, and each
   slice scored

Kosher salt

1 large zucchini, thinly sliced crosswise

1 red onion, thinly sliced into 8 slices

1 red bell pepper, seeded and thinly sliced into rings

½ cup extra-virgin olive oil

4 garlic cloves, chopped

½ cup assorted chopped fresh herbs, such as thyme, basil,
   parsley, oregano, and rosemary

1 tomato, cored and sliced crosswise into 8 slices

4 ounces soft goat cheese, such as Montrachet

Salt and freshly ground black pepper

8 cups baby spinach leaves

½ cup grated Parmesan cheese

In a 2-quart saucepan over medium-high heat combine the balsamic vinegar and honey. Bring to a boil, reduce the heat to medium-low, and simmer until the liquid is reduced to about ½ cup. This will take 25 to 30 minutes. (Watch during the last few minutes that the vinegar does not burn or scorch.) The reduction should be very thick, almost like molasses. Set aside to cool.

Preheat the oven to 400°F. Place the eggplant in a colander in the sink. Sprinkle with kosher salt and let drain for 30 minutes. Rinse the eggplant thoroughly, drain, and pat dry.

Place the eggplant, zucchini, red onion, and red bell pepper on 2 lightly oiled baking sheets.

In a small bowl combine the olive oil, garlic, and chopped herbs. Brush this mixture on the vegetable slices. Bake in the oven for 20 to 25 minutes, or until the vegetables are soft. Remove from the oven and allow to cool for 10 minutes. Leave the oven on.

Make 4 ratatouille tortes by stacking 1 slice of the eggplant, 2 or 3 slices of zucchini, 1 slice of red onion, a couple of rings of red bell pepper, 1 slice of tomato, and a couple of teaspoons of goat cheese. Repeat with remaining ingredients. Compress the tortes lightly with your hand. Season to taste with salt and pepper.

Place in the oven and bake for 8 to 10 minutes, or until the cheese begins to melt. Divide the baby spinach among 4 serving plates. Place a ratatouille torte in the center of each plate. Drizzle with the reduced balsamic vinegar and sprinkle with Parmesan cheese.

ROASTED PORTOBELLO, BRIE, & ARUGULA SALAD WITH LEMON PEPPER VINAIGRETTE

Botanically speaking, portobello mushrooms are just larger, darker versions of the common button variety. Because they are left to mature longer, they develop a heartier flavor and chewier texture. The U.S. Mushroom Council reports that they are all the rage these days: 30 million pounds of these giant mushrooms were consumed last year. With this recipe alone, I certainly ate my fair share of that amount.

SERVES 4

4 large portobello mushroom caps, stems discarded

2 tablespoons olive oil

1 (8 ounce) wheel of Brie, rind removed and discarded, cut into cubes, or a combination of Brie and Stilton cheese cubes

4 cups mesclun

4 cups arugula, stems removed

1 red onion, thinly sliced

2 fennel bulbs, cored and thinly sliced (chop and reserve the fronds for garnish)

⅓ cup freshly squeezed lemon juice

1 tablespoon grated lemon zest

2 garlic cloves, chopped

1 teaspoon Dijon mustard

1 teaspoon salt

2 tablespoons brined-cured green peppercorns, rinsed and drained

Sugar to taste

⅔ cup extra-virgin olive oil

Freshly ground black pepper

Preheat the oven to 375°F. Brush the portobello mushroom caps with olive oil. Place the mushrooms on a foil-lined baking sheet. Roast in the oven for 5 minutes. Remove from the oven and fill the mushroom caps with the Brie cubes. Return to the oven and bake for 8 to 10 minutes, or until the cheese melts. Remove the mushrooms to a wire rack to cool.

Divide the mesclun and arugula among 4 individual serving plates. Place a roasted mushroom cap in the center of each plate. Scatter the red onion and fennel slices on top.

Make the lemon pepper vinaigrette: In a small bowl whisk together the lemon juice, lemon zest, garlic, Dijon mustard, salt, peppercorns, sugar, and olive oil. Taste and adjust seasonings with additional salt or sugar if needed. Drizzle the vinaigrette over the salad and top with a few grindings of freshly cracked pepper. Garnish with chopped fennel fronds.

Variation: For a deep, smoky flavor, grill the mushroom caps over medium-hot coals for 3 minutes. Turn and fill with the cheese. Close the grill lid and continue cooking about 5 minutes, or until the cheese has melted.

SPAGHETTI SQUASH SALAD WITH ORANGE TAPENADE VINAIGRETTE

Spaghetti squash seems to be a big mystery for a lot of people, but I'm not sure why. It is delicious to eat, simple to prepare, and makes a beautiful presentation. This recipe is adapted from one of my favorite cookbooks (and an excellent culinary resource guide): Sweet Onions and Sour Cherries, *by Jeannette Ferrary and Louise Fiszer.*

SERVES 4

1 large spaghetti squash

1 cup pitted niçoise or kalamata olives

3 anchovy fillets

2 garlic cloves, chopped

2 green onions, chopped

2 tablespoons capers, rinsed and drained

1 tablespoon herbes de Provence

¼ cup chopped fresh basil

2 tablespoons chopped parsley

⅓ cup extra-virgin olive oil

3 tablespoons freshly squeezed lemon juice

Salt and freshly ground black pepper

½ cup oil-packed sun-dried tomatoes, drained and cut into thin strips

1 red onion, chopped

1 green bell pepper, seeded and chopped

1 cup diced smoked mozzarella

⅔ cup pine nuts, lightly toasted (see page 9)

½ cup freshly squeezed orange juice.

Grated zest of 1 orange

½ cup grated Romano cheese

Very thinly sliced French bread, lightly toasted

Preheat the oven to 400°F. Pierce the spaghetti squash several time with a fork. Place on a baking sheet on the middle rack of the oven and bake for 45 minutes to 1 hour, or until the squash is tender. Remove from the oven and allow to cool. When cool enough to handle, cut the squash in half lengthwise and scoop out and discard the seeds. With a fork, scoop the pulp out into a large bowl. It will come out in strands. Set aside.

While the squash is baking, make the tapenade: In a food processor combine the olives, anchovies, garlic, green onions, capers, herbes de Provence, basil, and parsley. Process until the mixture is very finely chopped, almost to a smooth purée. With the machine running, gradually add the olive oil and lemon juice in a thin, steady stream until the mixture is very smooth and paste-like. Season to taste with salt and pepper.

To the spaghetti squash add the sun-dried tomato strips, red onion, green bell pepper, smoked mozzarella, and pine nuts. Toss gently to combine.

In a small bowl whisk together ⅓ cup of the tapenade mixture with the orange juice and orange zest, reserving the remaining tapenade. Toss the vinaigrette with the vegetables. Divide the vegetables among 4 individual salad plates and sprinkle with Romano cheese. Spread the remaining tapenade over slices of toasted French bread and serve alongside the salad.

CRAB CAKES ON MESCLUN WITH JALAPEÑO REMOULADE DRESSING

Remoulade is a mayonnaise-based sauce found throughout the Cajun/Creole cuisine of Louisiana, with different regions supporting their own variations. I like this version a lot, but you can experiment by adding 1 to 2 tablespoons of the following, either alone or in combinations: prepared horseradish, chopped fresh ginger, Creole mustard, brine-soaked green peppercorns, or roasted garlic.

SERVES 4

1½ cups mayonnaise, divided

1 tablespoon anchovy paste

1 teaspoon dry mustard

2 garlic cloves, chopped

2 gherkin pickles, chopped

1 tablespoon capers, rinsed and drained

2 tablespoons chopped fresh dill

2 tablespoons freshly squeezed lemon juice

2 teaspoons Worcestershire sauce

½ teaspoon Tabasco, or to taste

1 jalapeño pepper, seeded and chopped

2 tablespoons butter

1 small red bell pepper, seeded and chopped

1 small onion, chopped

2 teaspoons Jamaican jerk seasoning or seafood seasoning

¼ cup chopped parsley

1 pound crabmeat, picked over

Salt and freshly ground black pepper

1½ cups cracker meal, divided

½ cup vegetable oil

10 cups mesclun

1 tablespoon olive oil

1 tablespoon balsamic vinegar

Paprika for sprinkling

In a large bowl combine 1 cup of the mayonnaise, anchovy paste, dry mustard, garlic, gherkins, capers, dill, lemon juice, Worcestershire, Tabasco, and jalapeño. Cover and chill.

In a 12-inch skillet melt the butter over medium-high heat. Add the red bell pepper and onion and cook until soft, about 5 minutes. Transfer the contents of the skillet to a large bowl. Wipe the skillet clean with a paper towel and set aside. Stir the jerk seasoning, the remaining ½ cup of mayonnaise, parsley, and crabmeat into the sautéed vegetables. Season to taste with salt and pepper. Stir in ½ cup of the cracker meal. The mixture should be moist, not dry. Place the remaining 1 cup of cracker meal in a shallow bowl or pie plate.

Take about ½ cup of the crabmeat mixture and shape into a small cake or patty. Coat in the remaining cracker meal. Repeat with the remaining crabmeat mixture. You should have about 12 crab cakes. Place on a parchment-lined baking sheet, cover, and refrigerate for 30 minutes. (The crab cakes can be made 4 to 6 hours ahead and chilled.)

Heat the vegetable oil in the skillet over medium-high heat until sizzling. Add the crab cakes, one at a time, to the hot oil. Fry the cakes, about 1 minute per side, turning once. Remove and place on paper towels.

In a large bowl toss the mesclun with the olive oil and balsamic vinegar. Season with salt and pepper. Divide the greens among 4 individual plates. Place 3 cakes in the center of each plate and spoon some of the dressing over each crab cake. Sprinkle with paprika. Serve at once.

WINTER WHITE SALAD WITH PAN-SEARED SCALLOPS

This is the traditional late-night supper I serve to a few close friends on New Year's Eve. The salad, vinaigrette, and scallops can be prepped ahead and assembled at the last minute—that gives me plenty of time to reflect on the past year and toast the new one.

SERVES 4

2 pounds sea scallops, patted dry

Salt and freshly ground black pepper

⅓ cup flavored olive oil (such as basil oil, chile oil, or rosemary oil)

Juice of 1 lemon

½ cup raspberry vinegar

1 teaspoon Dijon mustard

1 tablespoon sugar

1 tablespoon poppy seeds

¾ cup extra-virgin olive oil

12 cups mixed light-colored baby greens, such as bibb, Boston, romaine, frisée, and Belgian endive, torn into bite-sized pieces

1 cup sliced mushrooms

1 cup chopped walnuts, lightly toasted (see page 9)

1 cup fresh raspberries

Season the scallops with salt and freshly ground black pepper. Heat the flavored oil in a 12-inch skillet over medium-high heat. Add the scallops and sauté until cooked through, turning once, about 3 minutes. Drizzle with lemon juice. Transfer to a bowl and set aside.

Make the vinaigrette: In a small bowl whisk together the raspberry vinegar, Dijon mustard, sugar, ½ teaspoon of salt, 1 teaspoon black pepper, and poppy seeds. Add the olive oil in a thin, steady stream, whisking constantly until the vinaigrette is thick and emulsified. Set aside.

In a large bowl toss together the mixed greens and mushrooms. Divide the greens among 4 individual serving plates. Arrange the scallops on top of the greens. Sprinkle with chopped walnuts and raspberries. Drizzle with half of the vinaigrette, and pass the remainder separately. Serve with Stilton Croûtes (for recipe, see page 32.)

CHILI-RUBBED SALMON SALAD WITH CILANTRO CURRY VINAIGRETTE

This vinaigrette has a wonderful affinity for tropical fruit. You can substitute pineapple, mango, kiwi, starfruit, or papaya for the oranges.

SERVES 4

4 (6 to 8 ounce) salmon fillets

2 tablespoons chili powder

¼ cup freshly squeezed lime juice

1 tablespoon Dijon mustard

2 tablespoons honey

2 garlic cloves, chopped

1 tablespoon mild curry powder, preferably Madras

1 teaspoon cumin seeds

1 teaspoon salt

⅔ cup extra-virgin olive oil

⅓ cup chopped fresh cilantro

1 red bell pepper, seeded and thinly sliced crosswise into rings

1 green bell pepper, seeded and thinly sliced crosswise into rings

1 yellow bell pepper, seeded and thinly sliced crosswise into rings

1 red onion, thinly sliced

2 navel oranges, peeled, thinly sliced, and seeded

½ cup sunflower seeds, lightly toasted (see page 9)

Preheat the oven to 425°F. Rub the salmon fillets on both sides with chili powder. Place on a baking sheet that has been lined with heavy-duty aluminum foil. Bake in the oven for 8 to 10 minutes, or until the salmon flakes easily with a fork. Remove from the oven.

Make the cilantro curry vinaigrette: In a medium bowl whisk together the lime juice, Dijon mustard, honey, and garlic. In a small skillet set over medium heat, toast the curry powder, cumin seeds, and salt for 1 to 2 minutes, or until the spices become fragrant. Be careful not to scorch the spices, or the dressing will have a burned taste. Whisk the toasted spices into the bowl. Slowly drizzle the olive oil into the bowl in a thin, steady stream, whisking constantly until the dressing becomes thick and emulsified. Stir in the chopped cilantro.

On 4 individual serving plates layer the red, green, and yellow bell pepper slices with the red onion and orange slices. Place a salmon fillet on top and drizzle with vinaigrette. Sprinkle with sunflower seeds just before serving.

CAJUN ANDOUILLE & RICE SALAD WITH PECANS & FIG DRESSING

Spanish chorizo or hot Italian sausage work well if andouille is unavailable. This one-course entrée is the essence of the "Big Easy" — lusty, full of flavor, and the perfect excuse to get together with friends and let the good times roll!

SERVES 4

2 tablespoons vegetable oil

8 large andouille sausages, pricked all over with a fork

1 (12 ounce) bottle of beer (nonalcoholic is OK)

4 cups cooked white rice

1 red onion, thinly sliced

1 red bell pepper, seeded and thinly sliced

2 plum tomatoes, seeded and coarsely chopped

1 cup frozen green peas, thawed

2 carrots, shredded

1 cup thinly sliced mushrooms

1 cup pecan halves, toasted (see page 9)

¼ cup freshly squeezed lemon juice

1 teaspoon paprika

1 tablespoon Dijon mustard

2 garlic cloves, chopped

½ cup extra-virgin olive oil

1 teaspoon Tabasco

1 teaspoon salt

½ teaspoon black pepper

⅓ cup fig preserves

1 head romaine lettuce, separated into leaves

4 green onions, chopped

Heat the vegetable oil in a 12-inch skillet over medium-high heat. Add the sausages to the hot skillet and fry them, using tongs to turn them until well browned on all sides, about 10 minutes. Add the beer to the skillet, reduce the heat to medium, and cook, partially covered, for 15 to 20 minutes, or until the sausages are cooked through completely. Transfer the sausages to a plate lined with paper towels to drain.

In a large bowl combine the cooked rice, red onion, red bell pepper, tomatoes, peas, carrots, mushrooms, and pecan halves.

In a food processor combine the lemon juice, paprika, Dijon mustard, garlic, olive oil, Tabasco, salt, pepper, and fig preserves. Process until smooth and creamy. Pour over the rice mixture and toss to coat.

Line a large platter with romaine lettuce leaves and spoon the rice mixture over the lettuce. Nestle the cooked sausages on top and sprinkle with the green onions. Serve at once.

ROASTED SIRLOIN, POTATO, & MUSHROOM SALAD WITH ROQUEFORT DRESSING

I guarantee that even the most macho meat-and-potatoes guy cannot say no to this main-course salad.

12 medium-sized red new potatoes, scrubbed

½ cup olive oil

1 tablespoon chopped fresh rosemary

½ teaspoon salt

2 tablespoons balsamic vinegar

A 1½-pound sirloin steak, about 1 inch thick

1 tablespoon cracked black pepper

¾ cup sour cream

¼ cup mayonnaise

1 garlic clove, chopped

4 ounces Roquefort blue cheese, crumbled (about 1 cup), divided

4 green onions, chopped

Salt and freshly ground black pepper

6 cups mesclun

4 cups thinly sliced radicchio

1 Belgian endive, cored and thinly sliced lengthwise

1 pint cherry tomatoes, halved

1 red onion, thinly sliced

2 portobello mushroom caps, thinly sliced, or 1 cup sliced button mushrooms

Parmesan Garlic Croûtes (recipe follows)

Preheat the oven to 425°F. In a 2½-quart saucepan cover the potatoes with enough lightly salted water to cover them by 2 inches. Bring to a boil and cook for 8 minutes. Drain and refresh under cold running water. Quarter the potatoes. Place in a large bowl and toss with the olive oil, rosemary, and salt. Place the potatoes on a foil-lined baking sheet and bake until golden brown and tender, about 45 minutes. Stir every 10 minutes to facilitate even cooking. Remove from the oven and drizzle the potatoes with balsamic vinegar.

Turn the oven to broil. Rub the sirloin steak with the cracked black pepper. Place the steak on a broiler pan and place in the oven, about 6 inches from the heat source, and broil, turning once, about 3 minutes per side for medium rare. Remove from the oven and allow the steak to sit for 15 minutes before thinly slicing on the diagonal.

Make the Roquefort dressing: In a food processor combine the sour cream, mayonnaise, garlic, and half of the Roquefort. Process until smooth. Transfer to a small bowl and add the green onions and remaining Roquefurt. Season to taste with salt and pepper.

In a large bowl toss together the mesclun, radicchio, and Belgian endive. Divide the lettuce among 4 individual serving plates. Top each salad with some of the cherry tomatoes, red onion, and mushrooms. Lay the beef slices decoratively over the salad. Top with the roasted potatoes. Spoon the Roquefort dressing over the salad. Serve at once with Parmesan Garlic Croûtes.

PARMESAN GARLIC CROÛTES

8 slices of day-old French bread
⅓ cup olive oil
2 garlic cloves, minced
⅓ cup grated Parmesan cheese
½ teaspoon red pepper flakes

Preheat the broiler. Place the slices of French bread on a baking sheet. In a small bowl whisk together the olive oil, garlic, Parmesan cheese, and red pepper flakes. Brush the bread with the olive oil mixture. Broil for 1 to 2 minutes, or until the bread is toasted and the edges just begin to brown.

SKEWERED LAMB SALAD WITH HERB GREMOLATA DRESSING

For a special presentation and even more flavor, skewer the lamb on long branches of fresh rosemary.

SERVES 4

Juice of 6 lemons, divided

½ cup extra-virgin olive oil, divided

4 garlic cloves, chopped

2 pounds lamb shoulder, cut into 1-inch chunks, fat and gristle removed

Salt and freshly ground black pepper

¼ cup grated lemon zest

¼ cup grated orange zest

1 tablespoon Dijon mustard

1 tablespoon honey

½ cup chopped fresh mint

1 tablespoon chopped fresh rosemary

½ cup chopped pitted green olives

½ cup chopped pecans, lightly toasted (see page 9)

4 green onions, chopped

½ cup grated Parmesan cheese

10 cups mesclun

1 red onion, thinly sliced

2 roasted red peppers, thinly sliced

Lemon slices and mint sprigs for garnish

In a large glass bowl or zip-top freezer bag, combine half of the lemon juice, ¼ cup of the olive oil, garlic, and lamb. Place in the refrigerator and marinate for at least 3 hours, or overnight. Remove the lamb from the marinade and thread on 8 wooden skewers that have been soaked in water for 30 minutes to prevent them from burning.

Preheat the broiler or prepare the grill. Broil or grill the skewered lamb, 3 to 4 inches from the heat source, for about 6 minutes for medium rare, turning once. Remove from the heat and sprinkle with salt and pepper to taste.

Make the herb gremolata dressing: In a small bowl mix together the remaining lemon juice, the remaining ¼ cup of olive oil, lemon zest, orange zest, Dijon mustard, honey, mint, rosemary, green olives, pecans, green onions, and Parmesan cheese.

Divide the mesclun among 4 individual serving plates. Top each with red onion and roasted red pepper slices. Place 2 skewered lamb kebabs on each salad and spoon the dressing over the lamb. Garnish with lemon slices and mint sprigs.

SAUSAGE-STUFFED VIDALIA ONIONS WITH APPLE CIDER DRESSING

Don't let the list of ingredients discourage you from sampling this sophisticated salad. If you plan ahead, the onions can be stuffed a couple of days prior to serving, covered, and refrigerated, then baked while you are preparing the greens and the vinaigrette.

SERVES 4

1 pound hot Italian sausage

2 carrots, shredded

1 rib of celery, minced

1 yellow onion, minced

3 garlic cloves, minced

½ cup golden raisins

2 eggs, lightly beaten

1 cup seasoned stuffing mix, such as Pepperidge Farms (not cubed)

½ cup chicken stock

2 teaspoons poultry seasoning

Salt and freshly ground black pepper

4 large Vidalia onions, peeled and hollowed out with a melon baller, leaving ¼-inch shells

8 strips of bacon, chopped

1 tablespoon coarse-grained Dijon mustard

¼ cup honey

⅓ cup apple cider vinegar

¼ cup apple cider or juice

¼ cup walnut oil or olive oil

½ (10 ounce) package prewashed spinach leaves, stems removed (about 6 cups)

½ cup walnuts halves, toasted (see page 9)

Preheat the oven to 375°F. Butter an 8 x 8-inch baking pan. In a 10-inch skillet set over medium-high heat, crumble the sausage and cook it until it is browned completely, about 6 minutes. Drain and discard the drippings. Remove the sausage to a large mixing bowl. Add the carrots, celery, onion, garlic, golden raisins, eggs, stuffing mix, chicken stock, poultry seasoning, ½ teaspoon of salt, and ½ teaspoon of black pepper. Stir to thoroughly combine. Set aside.

Bring a 3½-quart Dutch oven filled with lightly salted water to the boil. Add the hollowed-out onions and blanch for 2 minutes. Remove with a slotted spoon and drain upside down on paper towels.

Divide the stuffing mixture among the onions, mounding the filling in the center. Place the onions in the prepared baking pan and bake for 30 to 40 minutes, or until the onions are golden and soft when pierced with a knife.

Meanwhile, make the apple cider dressing: In the same skillet used to cook the sausage, fry the bacon over medium-high heat until crisp. Remove with a slotted spoon to drain on paper towels. To the hot drippings add the mustard, ½ teaspoon salt, ½ teaspoon black pepper, honey, and apple cider vinegar. Bring to a boil and simmer for 1 minute. Remove from the heat and add the apple cider and walnut oil, whisking until thoroughly combined.

Divide the spinach among 4 individual serving plates. Place a stuffed onion in the center of each plate. Drizzle the dressing over the salad and sprinkle with walnut halves and reserved bacon. Serve at once.

ACKNOWLEDGMENTS

My name may be on the cover of this book, but there are many others behind the scenes who offer their wisdom, guidance, creativity, good humor, constant support, friendship, and love to me, every day. Everyone plays different roles and because of you, this book was made possible.

I gratefully acknowledge my parents, Jan and Ray Overton, for their wisdom and guidance; my brother, Ricky; my sister, Robyn; her husband, Tim; my nieces, Hope and Emma; my "Granny Lou"; and my "best buds," Gypsy and Cagney.

Thank you to my friend and culinary assistant, Susan Montgomery, to whom this book is dedicated. You are invaluable. And to my personal assistant and friend, Matt Ramsey, who makes my day-to-day life run smoothly, I appreciate you. And thank you to Nathalie Dupree for teaching me my craft in the first place.

To my editor, Suzanne De Galan, much love and appreciation for making every process of this book a joy. I admire your devotion, I praise your insight and your good common sense. I am fortunate to know you. Thank you Burtch Hunter, my talented designer. Words cannot express my gratitude. I am in awe of your talents, my friend. And special thanks once again to Chuck Perry, Steve Gracie, and Marge McDonald for continuing to support my writing endeavors.

Thank you to Brad Newton, my food photographer, who captured the images for this book. Your photographs are inspiring. And to his assistant, Susan Galligos, for doing everything in your power to make the photo session run smoothly. I appreciate my prop and food stylist, Lynne Mitchell. Each "picture setting" conveys the essence of the recipe, and I thank you. Special thanks to Michele Phillips for tirelessly assisting me at the shoot. You were a joy to work with. And again, heartfelt thanks to Vicky Murphy, Jim Laber, and Chris Rosenberger of Inland Seafood in Atlanta for providing the freshest and best seafood available for these images. Special thanks to eatZi's for the gorgeous greens used in the photographs.

I am grateful to Finn Schjorring and Faye Gooding of Le Creuset of America, Inc., for their constant support of my culinary projects, both with books and television production.

On a personal note, I want to thank my constant companions and friends to the end: Brian Seifried, Stephen Barnwell, Ken Folds, Clint Bearden, Allan Vineyard, Kenny Conley, Donald Alexander, Heyward Young, Kay Ponder, Nancy McKenna, Jeff Eisenberg, Virginia Willis, Will Deller, and Nancy Rogers. Here's to dreams coming true and many more good times together!

And finally, to the nearly 10,000 students whom I have been able to entertain and teach over the years: Your enthusiasm and desire to learn and better your personal world is what made *Main-Course Salads* a reality.

BIBLIOGRAPHY

Chesman, Andrea. *Salad Suppers: Fresh Inspirations for Satisfying One-Dish Meals.* Shelburne, VT: Chapter Books, Ltd., 1997.

Child, Julia. *The Way to Cook.* New York: Alfred A. Knopf, 1989.

Choate, Judith. *The Bean Cookbook.* New York: Kenan Books, 1992.

Corriher, Shirley O. *CookWise: The Hows and Whys of Cooking Revealed.* New York: William Morrow and Company, Inc., 1997.

Dupree, Nathalie. *Nathalie Dupree's Southern Memories.* New York: Crown Publishing Group, 1993.

Ferrary, Jeanette and Fiszer, Louise. *Sweet Onions & Sour Cherries: A Cookbook for Market Day.* New York: Simon & Schuster, 1992.

Herbst, Sharon Tyler. *New Food Lover's Companion.* New York: Barron's Educational Series, 1995.

Koplas, Norman. *Whole Meal Salads.* Chicago, IL: Contemporary Books, Inc., 1992.

McGee, Harold. *On Food and Cooking: The Science and Lore of the Kitchen.* New York: Scribner's Publishing, 1984.

McNair, James. *James McNair's Salads.* San Francisco, CA: Chronicle Books, 1991.

Miller, Mark. *The Great Chile Book.* Berkeley, CA: Ten Speed Press, 1991.

Overton, Ray. *Layers of Flavors.* Atlanta, GA: Longstreet Press, Inc., 1998.

Prudhomme, Paul. *Chef Paul Prudhomme's Louisiana Kitchen.* New York: William Morrown and Company, 1984.

Willan, Anne. *La Varenne Pratique: The Complete Illustrated Guide to the Techniques, Ingredients and Tools of Classic Modern Cooking.* New York: Crown Publishing Group, 1989.

INDEX

Parmesan, 55
pesto, 10
raspberry, 41
spicy pecan, 52
sun-dried tomato, 9
tarragon, 51
tart currant, 98
toasted cumin, 14
Warm Chicken Livers with Confetti Vinaigrette, 96
Warm German Potato Salad with Sausage and Caraway
 Vinaigrette, 76
White Bean Salad with Baby Shrimp and Tarragon
 Vinaigrette, 51
Winter White Salad with Pan-Seared Scallops, 105